NOW THAT I'VE GOT YOUR ATTENTION

The Story of Iva "Godiva" Larson

BY IVA LARSON
WITH SUSAN D. BRANDENBURG

This book was published in the U.S.A. by Susan the Scribe, Inc.

www.susanthescribe.vpweb.com

by Iva Godiva Larson

with Susan D. Brandenburg

Cover, Page Layout and Design:

Sally Sharp

www.sallyballsharp.com

ISBN: 978-1-7345165-9-3

TABLE OF CONTENTS

Don't wait for Valentine's Day to say I love you,
Christmas to give a gift, and New Year's Day to drink Champagne.
~ Iva Fran Larson

1

KEY WEST CONCHS AND OTHER RELATIVES

My mother was a 'Conch' (born in Key West, Florida). Both my older sister Sue (born in 1939) and I were named after Key West Conchs … our maternal grandparents, Sue Griffin Elwood and Ivan Elwood. Grandfather Ivan was the police chief in Key West for thirty years. His father had been a sea captain. Mother and her sister, Dorothea (Dot), ran away from home as teenagers and spent time in Miami before coming to Jacksonville in hopes of meeting sailors stationed at the Naval Air Station.

Mama found her sailor and married him. My parents, Robert Frank "Bob" Larson and Alberta "Bert" Audrey Elwood, met in a dancehall across from the Florida Theatre in downtown Jacksonville. Daddy had been in the South Pacific on a Navy Ship, The USS Arizona, and was transferred back to Jacksonville in November of 1941, just three weeks before the Japanese bombed Pearl Harbor and killed so many [1,177 sailors and Marines] aboard the USS Arizona. He always considered himself a lucky man.

Mama had a beautiful watch that Daddy gave her when he came back from being stationed in Hawaii on the USS. Arizona. It was rose gold with emeralds, diamonds and rubies. He talked about how he had made and sold sandwiches to the other sailors instead of going on leave so that he could save up money to buy her something beautiful. She treasured that watch, and I always treasured the fact that Daddy was so practical and frugal with his money. That is something he taught me that has really come in handy over the years. Unfortunately, that precious watch (although not really valuable monetarily, but irreplaceable sentimentally), along with several other special mementos, mysteriously disappeared about the same time that Sue and her family came through my house looking for keepsakes. It was shortly before I sold the Windsor Place house in Avondale, and I asked them to let me know what they wanted, as I don't believe in waiting to die before leaving things to loved ones. Sadly, no one asked or let me know what they were taking.

I was born on January 22, 1944, at St. Luke's Hospital in Jacksonville, Florida. It's coincidental that Jacksonville was once called "Cowford," and I spent much of my young childhood on a farm in Michigan, where Daddy grew up. Daddy always talked about going straight from the farm to the Navy at a young age, never having seen the ocean before joining up. On his first night watch on the ship, he pulled the fire alarm when he saw phosphorus on the waves. He thought the ship was on fire!

Daddy's father, Grandpa Larson, was a strong, gentle Swede. I remember sitting at his feet while he fondly stroked my long blonde hair. I was such a little towhead when I was a toddler and now that I'm "toddling again in my golden years," I'm going to remain a blonde for the rest of my life!

When we visited Grandpa Larson at the farm in Michigan, I asked him why he didn't have electricity and his answer was, "I go to sleep when it's dark and get up when it's light – why do I need electricity?" I spent several summers there as a girl and I remember how I enjoyed priming the pump and pumping the water and how I absolutely hated the nasty outhouse! Sometimes, Grandpa Larson would come to visit us in Jacksonville. He came to see us soon after I was born and we bonded instantly. He was a special Grandpa.

Daddy had one older brother, Uncle Otto, whom we nicknamed "Uncle Blotto" because

Grandpa Larson holding me, Mama and Sue next to us

he drank too much. Uncle Blotto lived in Las Vegas and once, when he was driving us, he stopped at all the green lights and ran the red lights.

When Daddy lost his mother to illness, he was only five or six years old. He learned to cook and sew and iron because his mother wasn't there anymore. Daddy became quite self-sufficient. There was nothing he couldn't fix or build. He was my ideal man and I set my standards high. I remember how shocked my first husband, Ed, was when I purchased the lumber and asked him to build me a bookcase. I just assumed that all men had the same skills that Daddy had … but soon discovered he was one of a kind. Daddy could even build a bicycle built for two!

After he got out of the Navy, Daddy worked as a manager at Sears, Roebuck for a while and then became an interior designer. He owned Larson's Interiors on Lomax Street in the Five Points section of Jacksonville. My mother, Bert Larson, also became an interior decorator and worked with Daddy. They became quite popular throughout the State of Florida, and I remember traveling to posh residences in South Florida with Daddy. I also vividly remember playing in the big display window of Larson's Interiors and how, one day just an hour or so after I stopped playing there, a woman pushed on her gas pedal instead of her brake pedal and rammed her car right through the window. I guess I inherited some of Daddy's good luck.

Daddy was down to earth and extremely considerate and polite - he was sought after because he had such a nice manner and such a wealth of talent. He decorated Anthony's Salon at the Commander Towers and later became Director of Housekeeping at St. Vincent's Hospital, decorating the patient rooms and the lobby, and making sure that the hospital was maintained in pristine condition.

One stellar characteristic of Bob Larson was his fairness. He was known in the community for his insistence upon equality for all citizens. He displayed this sense of fairness whenever he could and an example of that was when he acknowledged an African-American cleaning lady for her many years of service to St. Vincent's by assigning her Cleaning Cart #1. In the 1950's and 60's that was "just not done" in segregated Jacksonville. Daddy got so much guff from others on the staff for that simple act. I've always been so proud of the man he was.

**Daddy –
Robert Frank Larson**

Eleanor, an African-American lady, came and did the ironing for us regularly. She would play religious music on the radio and sometimes she brought her grandson. I was very young when she first brought him to the house and my parents talked about it later, that they found me licking my thumb. I had rubbed it on his arm and expected the color to come off, thinking he might just be made of chocolate!

My parents did everything they could to combat racial prejudice. Another example was when our church, Riverside Park Methodist, hosted a group of African Missionaries. There were no hotels in town where they could stay, so the congregation was asked to invite them into their homes. Only the Larson family opened their home to them. We lived on Windsor Place in Avondale at the time. It was a pretty upscale neighborhood. Our house was egged when our African guests were there.

I had an ideal childhood. As a girl in an upper middle-class family in Jacksonville during the postwar years of the 1940's and 1950's, I lived in a fairytale ... everything was just right. I took dance lessons and performed in recitals. My parents were always there for me, cheering me on.

When I say my parents cheered me on, I mean that they often actually set me up to success. For instance, when I was in Girl Scouts, I sold the most Girl Scout Cookies of anyone in town. I was known as the Cookie Queen and received a golden statue of a Girl Scout. The back story to this is that my parents fronted me by buying many boxes of cookies and I had them to resell at every opportunity. I was resourceful, always, and managed to sell more on my own than with my troop. I still have my five-year pin and my Girl Scout sash. Being a Girl Scout was a highlight of my young childhood.

I was raised at Riverside Park Methodist Church from the time I was a little girl. I so well remember the first time my parents took me to kindergarten Sunday School. The feeling I had when I turned around and they were gone was one of pure terror – I was so shy – I thought they were going to stay with me. Daddy would not allow me to let my shyness get the best of me, though. I remember there was a boy who lived across the street and was a bully. When I told Daddy the boy had hit me, he made me march right across the street and punch him back. The boy left me alone after that.

By the time I was in Y Teens at Church, I had learned a great deal about socializing and was still learning resourcefulness from Daddy. Again, as in Girl Scouts, my parents fronted me money by buying dozens and dozens of bags of potato chips for our Y Teen Fundraiser. I took those bags of potato chips to school and sold them to hungry kids for 25 cents. Needless to say, I was the Potato Chip Queen, and raised the most money for Y Teens that year. We had dancing in the gym during school and I kept changing partners to sell more potato chips. I was a hustler even then and I didn't know it. That's one of the reasons I was always a good fund raiser … I was not afraid to go after what I wanted.

We had a dog named "Cassnoodles," why I do not know. We called him "Cassi" for short.

I loved being Little Bo Peep

He was a mutt that we picked up in Michiagn. On the drive home, Daddy heard a scream. It was me. "The puppy bit me," I cried. Daddy said, "Bite him back." I did. Then the puppy cried. One day, when I was in kindergarten, Cassi followed me to school. I remember it vividly because Miss Runyan (who I called Miss Onion) was so terrified that she actually jumped up on her desk! She must have had some sort of horrible experience with a dog.

I remember being quite young when I saw Cassi laying limply in Daddy's arms as he gently placed him in the trunk of his car. I asked him, "Where's Cassi going?" and he replied, "Cassi is going to heaven."

Cassi and me

Mother's sister, Aunt Dot, was always a part of our lives when I was growing up and she remained a part of my life always. At one point, Aunt Dot's daughter, Lexa Lee Koonce, came and lived with my husband Ed and me in our New York apartment when she was between jobs. Ed was so patient and kind. He got to know all of my family, including the Key West branch. When Ed was in the reserves during the Cuban Missile Crisis, Ed and I visited in Key West. He met my Aunt Lily, an old woman who never cut her hair and my friend, Mel Fisher, the treasure hunter who had a museum about his discovery of the Atocha Shipwreck off of Key West.

*Give every day the chance to become
the most beautiful day of your life.
~ Mark Twain*

2

GROWING UP IN JACKSONVILLE

I first attended Bagley's Private School, a small pre-school where I learned ballet and tap dancing. I liked tap dancing best because it made noise. My parents went to every recital I was ever in and they always remembered the first dance recital at Bagley's because I spent my entire time in the center of the stage bent over trying to tie my ballet slipper. I was completely oblivious to the audience ... just concentrating on tying my slipper until the music stopped and the dance was over ... then I looked up and ran off-stage.

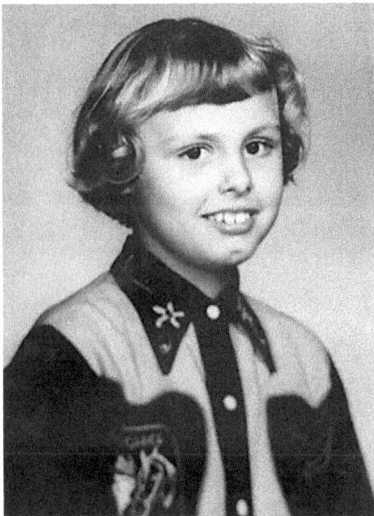

2nd Grade

After Bagley's, I attended Ruth N. Upson Elementary, John Gorrie Junior High and Robert E. Lee High School, graduating at age 16 because of my January birthdate.

When I was in elementary school, and all through my schooling even up through high school, I was painfully shy and quiet. I never considered myself super smart, but I was promoted quickly to the next grade and graduated early. My wanderlust probably started when I was at Ruth N. Upson Elementary and picked up a book about the Seven Wonders of the World. I was fascinated by the pyramids and knew that someday I would climb them.

As I mentioned, my parents were extremely active in our Riverside Methodist Church. Daddy loved to dress up as Santa Claus at Christmas and I remember he played Moses in a church play one year and I didn't recognize him in his costume. He was quite authentic with his beard and robe and staff. I actually

7

played Mary, the Virgin mother, in a manger scene at church one Christmas (I was quite authentically a virgin at the time … just in case you're wondering). Speaking of Christmas, we bought Daddy an electric shaver for Christmas when they first came out. It was under the tree and we were excited when he opened it until we noticed that some of his whiskers fell out of it. He had opened the package, used the shaver, rewrapped the present and put it back under the tree!

We were all quite involved in Sunday School and Youth Group. At Halloween, Daddy would sit on our front porch at Windsor Place and frighten kids who came trick or treating. He dressed up like a ghost and held the bowl of candy on his lap so that if they wanted candy, they had to come up to him and grab it out of the bowl.

Another thing my parents, especially Daddy, were known for in our church … they took in young Navy men and let them stay with us for the weekend. Daddy remembered when he was in the Navy in a strange port and didn't know anyone – so he and Mama went out of their way to make sailors comfortable and welcome in our church and our home. Before long, word got out in Mayport and NAS (Naval Air Station) that Riverside Park Methodist Church was a great place to make new friends, and there was even a family who would take them in for the weekend. A bonus was that the family featured two young blonde daughters. I treated all of the sailors like big brothers but later found out that my older sister Sue had some good times with some of them that were anything but "sisterly."

I was excited when I saw an ad for the Miss Jacksonville Pageant, September 22, 1962, first prize being a scholarship to Jacksonville University. That looked promising, so I went for it. By then, I was 17 and had graduated from high school. I had a couple of strange starts in my work-life … my first job was at H. H. Gage & Company on Forsyth Street, getting paid $15 per week for counting and sorting coffee beans … really. Then I got a job at Furchgott's Department Store downtown as a salesgirl, but "failed" at cash register training

IVA FRAN LARSON — Iva was born January 22, 1944 and is 18 years old. She graduated from Robert E. Lee High School in 1961. She is now taking voice lessons and dramatics. She would like to further her education at the Studio Theatre or the Music Center, and if this is not possible attend Jacksonville University. Iva stands 5 ft. 10½ in. and weighs 135 lbs. She has blond hair, brown eyes, and fair complexion. Her hobbies consist of designing clothes, bicycle riding, swimming, dancing, tennis, fencing, horse back riding, singing, acting and modeling.

and was demoted to gift-wrapping in the basement. By this time, I was nearly 6 feet tall, a slim natural blonde and I thought I might have a chance at that scholarship offered for the winner of the Miss Jacksonville contest. The winner would go on to compete in the Miss Florida Pageant and then, if she was chosen to be Miss Florida, she'd get to compete in the Miss America Pageant. Who knew what could happen, right?

Local broadcaster Dick Stratton was one of the judges and the contest was held at the George Washington Hotel Auditorium. I placed and got a nice little statue, but even though I didn't win the scholarship, it did lead to several local modeling jobs for me at Ivey's and Furchgott's Department Stores. Running for Miss Jacksonville was my first taste of modeling and it felt good … I knew I'd eventually pursue it more seriously, but first I had to make enough money to save toward my goals. In order to compete in Miss Jacksonville, I had to compete in several other contests, including the Miss Ocean State Bank contest.

My first and only "real" job was at Prudential Insurance Company. Not only was the Prudential Building the tallest high-rise in town, it was "the place" to work. I became an executive receptionist on the 8th Floor, working for Mr. Charles Campbell, and

attending Jacksonville University at night. I even got a delicious free lunch every day! Soon, I was asked to be Prudential's tour guide, taking visitors through the state-of-the-art building (golf putting green, library, etc.) and talking about the history of Jacksonville as well as the company. I learned a great deal about Jacksonville and really enjoyed being the tour guide. In later years, both the poise and the knowledge I gained by being a tour guide at Prudential served me well. Many times in my life I've been called upon to act as a hostess for people I did not know and it has always seemed to come naturally to me.

In my spare time, I volunteered as a docent for the Children's Museum in Riverside (now a bed & breakfast on what used to be called "Millionaire's Row"). I had been a tour guide for the Children's Museum since I was in middle school.

I worked at Prudential for about a year and managed to save $100, which was an impressive nest egg at that time. I took every opportunity that was offered me! The greatest opportunity was a trip to Europe sponsored by Prudential. We left on March 8, 1963, and traveled for three weeks, going to Lucerne, Milan, Venice, Florence, Rome, Genoa, Nice, Berlin, London and Paris, to name a few of the places we had the privilege of going. At the time, charm bracelets were the thing and so I bought a charm everywhere we went. I treasure that charm bracelet to this day and can reminisce whenever I look at the charms.

Iva Larson
Miss Ocean State Bank

My little piano charm is from Venice, where my roommate and I went into a piano bar and met four Army guys who offered us a gondola ride. We discovered, on closer inspection, that the Grand Canal in Venice was an open sewer with steps

leading down to the gondola thick with green moss and muck. The one soldier who had obvious designs on me was the unlucky one who slipped on those steps and fell. He climbed into the gondola cold and wet, covered with slime. I was not impressed. Later, after he dried off, we were sitting in the hotel lobby when he leaned over to me and said quietly, "I want to be alone with you." Everybody else had wandered off and we were sitting there by ourselves. I replied, "We are alone." I was still pretty naïve at age 19, but I did know he meant a bit more when he said he wanted to be alone with me.

My upbringing was old-fashioned. There were three main no-no's that had been drilled into my head always. 1) You didn't kiss on the first date. 2) You didn't have sex with a man unless you planned to marry him. 3) You never bragged or acted superior to anyone. So, with those rules firmly in place, I made it through Europe unscathed by scandal. My charm bracelet is now a necklace and still fascinating fodder for great memories. I can look at it and remember going to the Vatican, the Coliseum, Trevi Fountain, Eiffel Tower, Monaco, the Arch de Triumph, the German Beer Gardens, the Tower of London, the Spanish Steps, and, of course, the charms that are scattered throughout are the beautiful coins from each country.

The first time I went to Milano, Italy and visited La Scala – the opera house – it was on the organized Prudential trip. That first trip to La Scala, I was up on the top floor with the truck drivers. They had a pole that you could hold on to and lean out to see the stage. I was thrilled to be there! When I returned to La Scala several years later, I was sitting down on the front row. I loved both experiences and was

11

thankful for them. I have fun one way or the other. I've flown the Concord from Paris to New York City and I've flown coach – both were enjoyable.

After competing in Miss Jacksonville and taking my trips to New York and to Europe, I knew I wanted to be a model and that New York was the place to do it, so I informed my parents I had a New York City Map and $100 and I was taking the train to meet my future. My parents were not happy about my plans, but I was 19, invincible and couldn't wait to get started as a model.

Be an unshakeable optimist.
Concentrate on one thing at a time.
Practice self-discipline.
Do what you should do, when you should do it,
whether you like it or not.
~ Thomas Huxley

3

NEW YORK – WHERE LIFE TRULY BEGAN!

I moved into the Ferguson Residence for Women on 68th Street. The rent was $30 a week, and there were no men allowed above the first floor. I could see the Chrysler Building from my window and spent many nights gazing out the window and crying myself to sleep after a long day of pounding the pavement from modeling agency to modeling agency. I was such a hay seed, I didn't even have a portfolio of photographs!

One day I saw an ad in the paper about Jantzen Swimwear hiring models in the garment district. I bought a Saks 5th Avenue outfit on sale and walked in with an air of confidence that I didn't really have. What I did have, though, was the "Larson Luck."

A chic receptionist with a British accent greeted me and ushered me into the office of Mr. John Hamilton. I later discovered that John Hamilton was from Spokane, Washington and had two daughters. I reminded him of one of his daughters and he could tell that I was a small town girl and totally naïve. I got the job and Mr. Hamilton became my protector.

The Jantzen Swimwear job was my ticket to success. Soon, I moved uptown, sharing a brownstone apartment at 19 E. 76th Street with two roommates, who were secretaries.

My parents were worried about me being lonely and alone in New York City, so they sent me a little Pekinese puppy in a basket. My future husband Ed (who was going to law school in New York City) named him Sebastian after a character in a book he was reading.

I discovered when I was working with Jantzen that there were many "Summer Bachelors" lurking around photo shoots and the studio. They were men who stayed in New York City while their wives and kids went to the shore for summer vacation. Models were prime targets and these guys were on the prowl. That was when Mr. Hamilton (my boss and guardian angel) let me bring Sebastian, my Pekinese, to work in my tote bag. Sebastian wouldn't let anyone near me. When I was working, he stayed on a chair in my dressing room … usually. One day, I heard Mr. Hamilton's booming voice, "IVA! Sebastian's been in my office! That's not a tootsie roll on my carpet!"

My mother came to New York City for my 21st birthday. I was at work and had ordered a chicken dinner to be delivered for her. Unfortunately, when she answered the door, thinking it was the chicken delivery, a bunch of movers walked in and hauled off all the rented furniture. The landlord of the brownstone had not paid the rental fee for the furniture and it was being repossessed. My roommates and I came home to a bewildered lady from Jacksonville sitting in an empty apartment eating a chicken dinner!

When I lived in the East Village, the subway tokens were 15 cents. I had a good check waiting for me over at Madison Avenue and 76th Street, so I went to the subway man and told him I had a check at my agency, but I didn't have money for

a token. I said, "If you loan me the token, I'll pay you when I get back." He loaned me the token.

I later moved up town to an apartment on 46th Street, next to the U.N., between 2nd and 3rd Avenue. In my spare time, I became a tour guide for the United Nations, and learned interesting facts to tell tourists, such as the fact that Manhattan is an Indian word for "Island of Hills."

When I first got to New York, I was tall and thin, nearly devoid of breast or butt, however, because the camera adds weight, I was constantly being told I needed to lose weight! That wasn't difficult because I did a great deal of walking from job to job and there were times when I had so little money that I was making soup out of the ketchup packets. My roommates and I would buy a dozen eggs and put our names on the eggs. They were three flight attendants and me, the model. Each of us had fabulous dates, but no money. When we went out on a date, we ate and took left-overs home for the "dog!" The flight attendants would bring home filet mignon in the unused barf bags from the flights. We had to be resourceful. We had one bedroom and wall to wall beds. When we first moved in together, I was thinking it wouldn't be too crowded because they'd be flying, but it seemed like we were all there at the same times often.

Soon after we moved in, I decided to be friendly, have an open house and meet our neighbors. I put invitations under everybody's door on my floor. I was unaware that our

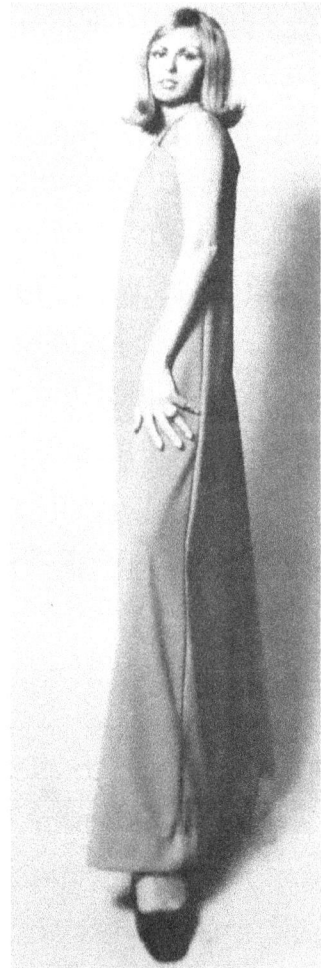

And they wanted me to lose weight!

17

nearest neighbor was a hooker with an angry black pimp. The police were called because word got around about the open house. The policeman asked, "Who's in charge here?" I admitted it was me and he told me, shaking his head, "They're still coming up the street!" I discovered that New York City is not the place to have an open house. The apartment was packed. It was my last open house in New York.

The Carlyle Hotel where Jackie Kennedy was known to go in the evenings to listen to Bobby Short's music on the piano bar was right across the street from my apartment. I often saw John and Caroline Kennedy with their secret service men in the Madison Avenue Deli. I got my hair done at Kenneth's, where Jackie Kennedy got her hair done. I was definitely moving on up!

I became the Southeastern promoter for Jantzen Swimwear, appearing in radio and television interviews and commercials. Here I was modeling in Central Park and making $50 an hour! I realized later that the dogs were making more than I was.

Finally, I moved into my own apartment at 37 King Street in the Village. It was on the first floor and had no air conditioning, but Sebastian and I loved it. The first floor is generally not a safe place to be, but I had an advantage in that the Italian Mamas lived in that building. They would sit out on their chairs during the day, and they took me in. It turned out, they were the Mafia wives. The Mafia mistresses were uptown on the Eastside. I was completely safe – never broken into – never in danger. That King Street location was carefully guarded, and it was in a great location. Ed was going to NYU and he'd pick me up on his motorcycle for dates. I also went on dates to theater parties and operas at Lincoln Center. It was an education and I was all for adventure.

A cast of my body was used as the model for the Saks 5th Avenue mannequin … how I wish I had one of those mannequins to place in the corner of my living room now! I marvel that I was the body for Saks Fifth Avenue mannequins in New York!

Speaking of casts, I do have a life mask of my face in my living room. In 1986, I went to the New York studio of Willa Shalit, daughter of film critic Gene Shalit, and sat for her as she created a life mask of my face. She prepared a mold of plaster gauze and applied it to my face, allowing it to set for about fifteen minutes. It was not comfortable, but I sat, immobilized with my eyes and mouth closed, breathing through my nose. She removed the mold and did her magic. She developed the use of an "inner image of the mask," a true art form of three-

Cast by Willa Shalet

dimensional beauty that appears to be alive. Today, that life mask graces my living room and, like the many photographs in my home, it reminds me of days gone by.

Willa Shalit's "Cast List" is impressive. Among the luminaries who have had their life masks casted by Shalit are Muhammad Ali, William F. Buckley, Jr., Richard Burton, Sammy Davis, Jr., Farrah Fawcett, Whoopi Goldberg, Federico Fellini, Helen Hayes, Sophia Loren, Paul Newman, Presidents Richard M. Nixon and Ronald Reagan, Isaac Stern, James Taylor, Robin Williams, and so many more ... including yours truly ... Iva Godiva Larson!

As a model, I had the privilege of meeting many celebrities, including Gloria Steinem and others, and became a model for the Willamina Agency, appearing in McCall Magazine. As the years went by, I appeared in television commercials in New York, Philadelphia and around the world. I was once in a skit on the Johnny Carson Show with Ed McMann and Johnny in New York. It was fun meeting them!

In New York, if you're a model or an actress, you're also usually a bartender or a waitress to make

New York Model

ends meet. I didn't want to do either of those things, so I did trade shows and they paid well. Every job was different. For GE, I had a portable organ hanging around my neck and I walked through the trade show playing the organ. Another time, back when Star Wars was popular, my costume was all silver from head to toe, with high silver boots and a cap attached to my head. It was wild. They had a room with music playing from the new Star Wars movie and I was just supposed to stand there like a mannequin.

At Lord & Taylors, I actually was a live mannequin, standing in the window for 15 to 20 minutes at a time. I had a lot of fun with that job because people would come up and look closely and say, "She looks real." I'd wait until someone was touching me and then I'd take a break. It scared the wee-wee right out of them!

Modeling is not for people with thin skin…models shed many tears. You can go to twenty "Go-sees" and be rejected every time. I remember consoling a young model who was new to the profession. She was crying because she'd been told she was too young. I told her that I'd been told I was too old. Modeling was hard work but extremely exciting and I loved the opportunities I had for new experiences – like getting into a helicopter on the roof of the Pan Am Building in Midtown Manhattan and flying over Niagra Falls … how many people get to do things like that? It was a magnificent sight and I had the privilege of riding in helicopters more than once.

I used to hang out at a couple of discos in New York – Le Club, Regine's and others – once in a while. I met a man at LeClub named Huntington Hartford, the heir of the A & P fortune. Huntington would hang out by the ladies room to meet women. He wasn't really a creep, but he was older and I wasn't interested in him at all. He came after me and wouldn't give up. I wouldn't give him my address or my phone number but somewhere in a conversation, I had slipped and said I

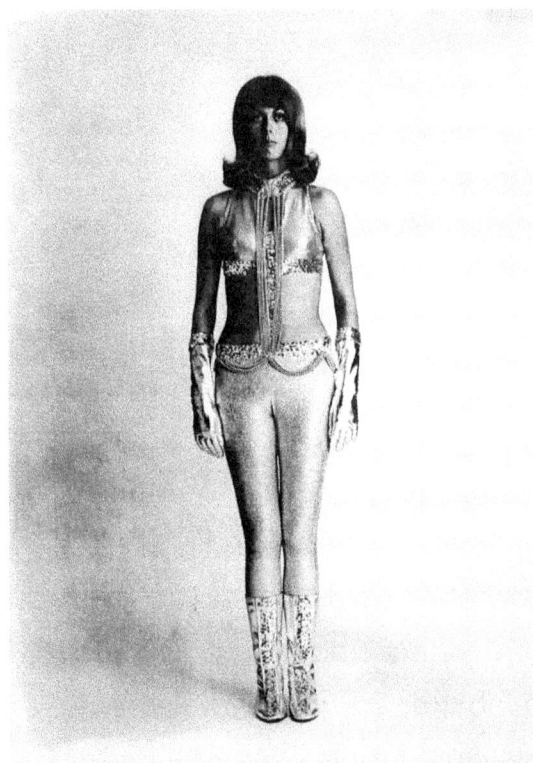

Just another day at the office

21

lived on 44th Street. I found out later that he had his chauffeur drive all the way up and down 44th Street – East and West – a long trek - and stop at every building and talk with every doorman until he found my apartment, which he did. Huntington lived on Sutton Place – a very expensive area overlooking the river. He invited me to a party at his apartment and I figured there was safety in numbers, so I walked there from my apartment on East 44th. I used to walk everywhere in Manhattan, or bicycle to different places and study them, read about them and learn about the city.

When I walked into Huntington's apartment, he had a huge plastic garbage can right in the middle of his beautiful, well-appointed living room. Strange. He offered me a drink but I didn't drink, or if I did take a drink, I generally poured it into a planter. A weird group of people were in attendance at the party, including Huntington's very young girlfriend and her puppy. Her puppy was not trained and peed on Huntington's sofa. He got mad and knocked the puppy to the floor, where it broke a leg. Then the whole party was in an uproar about getting the poor little puppy to the vet. I left and went on home. It was just one of my many Manhattan adventures. I was asked out to dinner or invited to parties by so many men in those years, and I often accepted the invitation, but it never went further than dinner, the party or the play. This was due to my upbringing and also due to the fact that I was in love with my future husband, Ed, who was going to law school and still lived with his parents. I knew we would marry someday after he graduated, but in the meantime, New York was an exciting place and I loved going out with interesting people to expensive places that were certainly not in my budget. Ed didn't mind. We'd see one another when either of us had time, but his studies came first.

Once in a while, in my whirlwind of modeling in New York, I would go home to Jacksonville and visit my family. On one such visit early on in my career, I experienced what I can only call a "Doris Day Date." Here's how it happened:

I was in Jacksonville and met a nice man through friends. He was quite a bit older, probably in his early 40's and nice-looking. He owned his own insurance company and he invited me to go out to lunch with him. I always thought of lunch as a safe date. He picked me up and I introduced him to my parents, whose house rules I respected when I was visiting – including their 11 o'clock curfew (which wasn't much of a challenge since they rolled up the sidewalks in Jacksonville by 11 p.m. anyway).

My date started driving to the airport and I thought maybe I missed a new restaurant opening at the airport. He drove up to his private plane. "What are we doing?" I asked. He said, "I thought we could have lunch in Palm Beach." He was the pilot and we flew to Palm Beach to a private club. The first person I saw at the pool was George Hamilton. It was a lovely lunch. Then he said, "I thought it would be fun to go to Nassau for the weekend." I told him I couldn't do that – I only had what I had on. He said, "Don't worry about it. You can get anything you need when we're there." I called my parents and told them I was going to the islands for the weekend. I assured them he seemed like a nice guy. Very polite. Daddy said, "Use your own judgment."

It turned out that he was a gambler. I don't gamble because I never win. We flew in and they had beautiful, elegant, expensive shops at the hotel. He said to go in and sign for anything I wanted. I was very careful and I got a conservative navy blue two-piece knit skirt and a blouse and a bathing suit. We each had our own suites and he told me to go to my suite and he'd meet me at dinner. I was raised that you don't kiss on the first date and you don't have premarital sex with anyone you're not planning to marry. It was corny, particularly with the reputation my profession had, but that was me. So, I went to my suite with my new clothing and met him for dinner. That first night at dinner, he gave me a beautiful string of pearls to go with my outfit.

We had a lovely dinner and then he wanted to gamble. So, the first night, he gave me a couple of hundred dollars in chips and said, "Here – have fun. I'll be gambling until late. Go to your room anytime you want to." It took me less than 20 minutes to lose my chips, and I thanked him for a lovely evening and went to bed. I got up in the morning and went water skiing and took advantage of all the amenities while he slept late. We met for lunch and went sailing and then had dinner. After dinner, he gave me chips and went to gamble all night again. I lost the chips again and went back to my suite.

He said I could use the phone to call anyone I wanted to call. I sat in my suite and called friends in New York and my parents in Jacksonville. After two days and two nights, we flew back to Jacksonville. He had been a perfect gentleman. He apparently was not interested in a one-night stand. I think he may have been looking for a marriage partner. The next day, I got a gorgeous arrangement of white long-stemmed roses delivered to our house. I think the white must have been for purity. I went back to New York, and we corresponded a couple of times, but nothing ever came of it except that I had experienced a Doris Day Date that I will never forget!

I had a memorable date, also, that I called The Date From Hell … but I was the date from hell – not the man! My date was a wealthy man with a fancy sports car and a yacht, both of which I nearly destroyed in one day through a series of freak accidents! Nevertheless, he still asked me out again and even introduced me to his family. I couldn't believe it! I was never serious about the man, although he pursued me despite my carelessness with his "toys." Many years later, he looked me up and called, saying, "What ever happened to us?" US? As far as I was concerned, there never was an US!

Ever has it been that love knows not its own depth
until the hour of separation.
~ Kahlil Gibran

4

LOVE LOST

I was working at Prudential when I met a handsome Navy man, Edward Harry Duggan, Jr., at a party. He later took me on a tour of the destroyer at Mayport where he was a gunnery officer, and I was smitten. I was just 18 years old and he was so tall, dark and handsome that he could have been a model. He was smart and funny and we got along so well. I soon found myself writing on scrap paper, "Mrs. Edward Harry Duggan, Jr." I dated many men after Ed and I met, and had some great adventures, such as my Doris Day Date, but my doodles at Prudential were prophetic, as I was destined to become Mrs. Edward Harry Duggan, Jr. a few years later.

Ed and me ... young and beautiful

25

Ed had just graduated from the Naval Academy when we met. He was on his first tour of duty. I remember when we first met, I discovered that Ed was a generous man. He had a beautiful red Alpha Romeo and he loaned it to his supply officer, who wrecked it. It was never the same after that. We pushed it as much as we drove it, but we loved that car and we loved each other.

After getting out of the Navy, he went to law school and lived in Brooklyn, New York with his parents. While he was going to law school, he also worked as a basketball coach. He came from an Irish Catholic family and his mother went to mass every day at 6 a.m. They were very strict Catholics – Fish on Friday, etc. We were both dating other people for a few years, but I loved Ed. I knew there were women after him because he was so handsome, but he lived with his parents and went to school or worked all the time. When we started dating seriously, his mother thought I was the devil incarnate because I was Protestant. His parents did come to Jacksonville for our wedding. They stayed at Windsor Place with my family and were probably impressed by it, but not with the fact that we were Protestant. We had both a Protestant minister and a Catholic Priest officiating at the wedding ceremony.

My parents loved Ed. Daddy even put up a basketball hoop in our driveway for him. Ed was the son he never had. Ed was easy to love. They bonded in the garage over beer – he had a great sense of humor and loved to drink. I joked with

him when he passed his bar exam after law school, saying I was surprised, since he'd never "passed a bar" in his life.

When we finally decided to get married, I designed my own wedding gown. It was a simple design – modest – nothing flashy. I drew pictures and waved my hands and bought the material and my friend, the British receptionist from Jantzen, who was also a talented seamstress, created my dress. It was beautiful in its simplicity. I wore no jewelry … mainly because I had no jewelry. We had simple gold bands – no diamond engagement ring for me. Ed was just out of law school and I wasn't making a big salary at the time. I just had enough to pay for our wedding and that was it. Daddy and mother didn't have a lot of money either. There were some wedding showers put on by friends here, but all in

all, it was not a fancy wedding.

Ed and I were married at St. Paul's Catholic Church at Park & King and had our reception at the Officers Club at the Naval Air Station.

Ed stayed in the Reserves after we were married. He spent one weekend a month on shipboard.

After he graduated from New York University Law School and we were married, Ed joined a prestigious Admiralty Law Firm – Hill, Betts, Yamaoka, Freehill and Longcope, with offices located on the 52nd Floor of the World Trade Center. Ed was made a junior partner. Mr. Ellis, the senior partner, had an apartment on Park Avenue near the Waldorf Astoria and often invited us there.

One day, an important client visited Ed's Firm and I came in for lunch at the Club on the 52nd Floor that day. Mr. Gin, the important client, was Asian and didn't speak much English. When he saw me walk in, he sucked in his breath and said to Ed, in a heavy accent "Hot Pants!" (Hotta pantsa). After lunch, I offered Mr. Gin a ride back to his hotel. I was driving my Ducati motorcycle and I had an extra helmet for Mr. Gin. He was thrilled, however, it turned out his legs were too short to reach the pedals on the back and he had to hold on to me for dear life! I wasn't aware of his dilemma and took him the "scenic route" through Central Park. Despite his terrifying

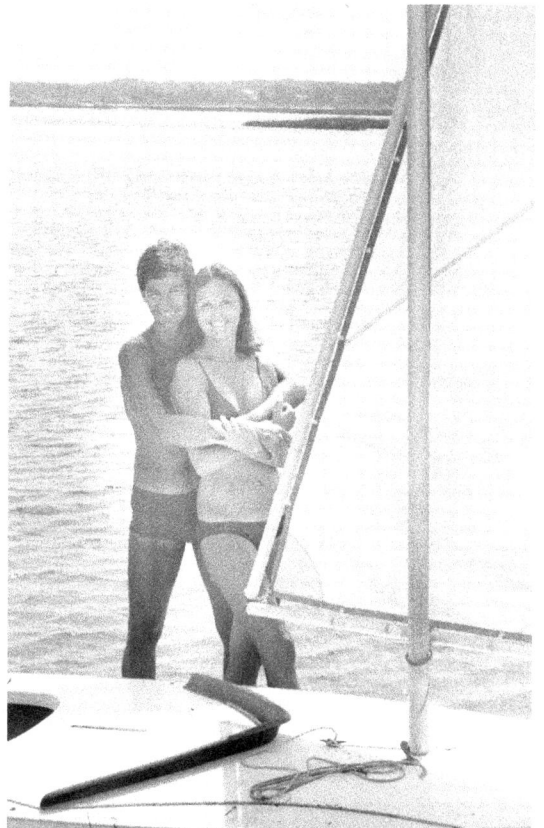

ride to his hotel, he insisted on spending time with Ed and me the rest of his visit, rather than the senior partners.

Speaking of motorcycles, I started driving a motorcycle when I was still in Jacksonville working at Prudential. It was much cheaper than a car and I loved the feel of it. I always wore a helmet, and with the exception of going on a couple of big expressways in New York, I was a safe driver most of the time. My parents wouldn't let me ride a motorcycle, so I used to drive the car to the Willow Branch Library and get on my motorcycle there. I drove a motorcycle most of the years that I modeled in New York, both before and after I married Ed.

Motorcycle driver!

Ed was drop-dead gorgeous and I was modeling – we looked like a celebrity couple whenever we walked into a place, and we were quite popular. In addition to his looks, Ed was valuable to the firm. The senior partners needed him. He could read a ship's log and tell if it was a lie – he loved to crawl into the belly of ships, and he had a rare quality for a New York attorney – he had integrity. As a junior partner, he didn't have a secretary, so after people went home at 5 o'clock, I'd go down to his office and type for him. I also decorated his office. I bought his desk at a furniture store on 5th Avenue and had drapes custom made. The senior partners' offices paled in comparison, and they brought clients in to see Ed's office!

When we first got married, we lived on the 8th Floor of an apartment building in

Manhattan and our next-door neighbors were Dirk and Ellen Brouwer. All of us were newlyweds and one couple on our floor had a honeymoon baby. We all did things together. Ellen called me "The life of the floor," probably because I was modeling and traveling … going to boat shows and trade shows and modeling for Jantzen swimwear. Sometimes, I'd bring home bathing suits I'd modeled and show them to Ellen – in fact, whenever I had an unusual costume to wear at a trade show, I'd usually show it off to my neighbors either before or after the show. I loved entertaining people with my adventures … it was fun telling stories and seeing them laugh. I was also the party giver of our floor – whatever the excuse, Ed and I had a party and invited an eclectic group of friends to our apartment. Remembering those days, Ellen said, "Iva would have a party at the drop of a hat. She told me all you needed was a bowl of peanuts and some drinks, and voila … a party!"

When we recently reconnected, Ellen and I talked at length about the time that I broke my leg skiing, and how amazing it was that Ed carried me around in his arms for weeks and weeks while I healed. We had been on the last run of the day on the ski slopes of Vermont when I fell and broke my tibia. It was a terrible break because I am all legs. I was placed in a heavy cast above the knee to my toes and it took me almost nine months to completely heal. I told Ed, "I could have had a baby in this time!" When I ventured out of our apartment, which wasn't too often, but often enough, I had to hail a big box taxi and put my leg out of the window because I didn't fit in it otherwise. When I look back at riding the motorcycle with Ed – it was insanity. I had the doctor who treated the New York Jets football team, so I was in good hands and probably would have healed more quickly if I had followed all instructions instead of being foolhardy. The doctor was Italian and always wore a flower in his lapel, but he didn't make my healing any easier. After the cast finally came off, I had a metal rod and ugly black shoes and a cane for what seemed like forever. I remember Ed and I once went to the coliseum when I was in a wheelchair … embarrassing. Also … I had told my friend, Florrie Glasser, that I would dance at her wedding and somehow, I did dance in spite of the metal rods and ugly black shoes. It was not a pretty sight.

Once, Ellen and Dirk rented a house near Quantico, Rhode Island and asked us to visit them. We came out on the train – me in my huge leg cast – and Ed carried me around on the beach. He was a joker and when he picked me up, he acted like he was going to throw me in the ocean, but I knew he was just kidding, like when he threatened to throw Sebastian out the window of our 8th floor apartment. Even though I knew he was kidding about Sebastian and I smiled, I didn't like that at all – Sebastian was my baby! Actually, Ed loved that little dog.

The Navy was something Dirk Brouwer and Ed had in common. Dirk had been in the Navy for three years and was an insurance broker when we were next door neighbors. The two of them made friends with John Witherspoon, and we all partied together. A funny thing that Ellen remembered was when the couple with the honeymoon baby moved to the suburbs … we went to see them and "shocked the suburbs," as we were a pretty wild bunch. Ellen always thought of me as "New York Born and Bred," although I was actually just a Florida girl at heart.

Ed and Sebastian

Ellen also remembered how I used to get bargains as often as possible. I always tried to save money, like when I told her about a special place to get our hair done for $5.00. Actually, it was a studio where they just massaged our heads, but for $5.00, it was a most marvelous thing to go after a long day of work and get your head massaged. I was always finding people to do facials and other services at a cheap rate, and when I could, I shared those experiences with my friends. Ellen worked for Bloomingdales when I first met her and then later for the Virginia State Travel Service as a travel counselor. Once, she and Dirk invited us to Fairfax, Virginia and we had dinner at the Red Fox Inn. We had some good times together.

As you know, my Dad was an interior decorator and once when Dirk and I were talking, Dirk remembered being on a ship in Jacksonville. It turned out that my father had redesigned the wardroom on this Navy ship for the officers and had redone the paneling. Dirk had actually met Dad when he was in Jacksonville. It's a small world.

A memory that we laughed about was that sometimes when I got home from a trip at 2 a.m., she and Dirk would hear hangers rattling in my closet next door and they'd say, "Iva's home." Sometimes, just to unwind, I'd run the vacuum ... they heard that, too. I must not have been as good a neighbor as I thought I was! Ellen also remembered Ed and I riding off on our motorcycle – both of us wearing formal clothing on our way to something glamorous. She called us "Quite the adventurers" ... and we were!

Ed was as much a fashion icon as I was. He wore a 41 extra-long and there weren't many stores that carried that size. When I walked into Saks, they'd meet me at the door because they knew I was buying clothes for my husband. He had several beautiful silk ties. Ed once said, "Iva, you pay more for my ties than I ever paid for my suits." The receptionist at the firm loved Ed and one day, a Greek tycoon walked in who needed an attorney – she took him back to Ed. Ed never lost a case. He charged by the hour instead of on contingency – had he charged by contingency, the check would have been unbelievable, but Ed was honest and fair – a good Irish Catholic boy. The Greeks, who flocked to him when they found out he charged by the hour, were not known for their honesty. He went to the office of one of his Greek clients and the receptionist told him he wasn't there. Ed knew he was there, so he walked around the receptionist and went into the office. The Greek was hiding on the floor under his desk – a grown man in a suit and tie under the desk! He knew Ed had caught him in a lie and he didn't want to be confronted. He came out from under the desk and shook hands with Ed. He tried to make small talk and said, "Where did you go to school?" Ed replied that he'd gone to the Naval Academy. The man's face fell. He said, "Oh, they go by the code of honor, right? You don't lie. Ever."

Speaking of Ed's reputation for honesty, our old friend Robert "Bob" Meshel was a trial attorney in an opposing law firm and was generally unpopular with opposing attorneys due to what Bob calls his "acerbic personality." Bob's friendship with Ed was unusual. Ed was a delightful guy," Bob said, remembering one particular "Salvor" case which took them to Key West. Ed was representing the ship owner and Bob was representing the other side – and since it involved a trip to the Florida Keys, the two attorneys decided to bring their wives and make it a semi-vacation. "Ed was my one weak spot," admitted Bob. "There were few people I loved as adversaries, but Ed was the exception." They negotiated a settlement on the salvor case in Key West, and the Meshels were introduced to new, unfamiliar foods such as conch, and shown around her old stomping grounds by Iva. He recalled that we were "a delightful couple," and I always had a smile on my face. Years after the Florida trip, Bob asked Ed to be one of his arbitrators, thinking that would be an

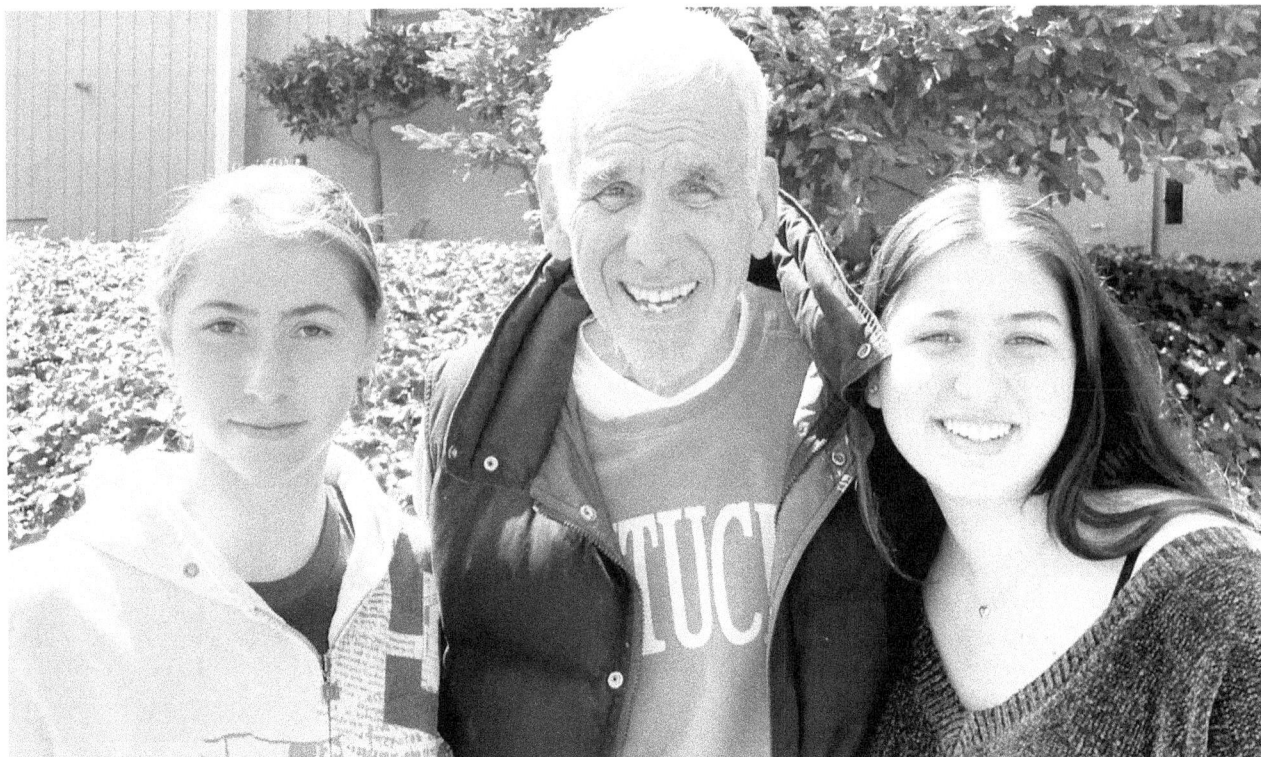

Bob Meshel and granddaughters

easy vote in his favor, but he was wrong. "The S.O.B. was honest!" complained Bob. "I couldn't count on him to vote in my favor."

Bob remembered that he and his wife, Miriam, came over to our apartment for dinner and ate my specialty, "Iva Du Dah." Actually, my specialty at the time was lasagna, but I called it "Swedish Lasagna" because I am a Swede. I'm also known for my frugality. Whenever I could pick up something on sale, I would, and I once picked up a few cans of tomato paste at a great price. I was busy fixing Swedish Lasagna, opened one of the tomato paste cans and it exploded! Red tomato paste everywhere! Now, that was definitely an Iva Du Dah Day!

Bob talked at length about Ed and Sebastian. He said, "Ed told me that every time Sebastian peed on the carpet, he would pick him up and put him on the turntable of the record player and spin him around for a couple of hours." Ed's disdain for Sebastian was pretty well known by all of our friends and neighbors, but he loved to play it up, too. He loved to joke around and Sebastian came in handy.

Ed and I had some wonderful and memorable times together, especially when we traveled to Ireland (Manor Hamilton, County Leetrum) to meet his family. As we were introduced to them, I'd hear whispers going around … "ooh, look at the size of her!" Ed had an older brother, Francis, and a younger brother, Gordon. His mother grew up in a tiny Irish village and we found the house where she grew up – there was a confirmation photo of his brother, Francis, there that she had sent back to Ireland, and temperance buttons on the table.

Ed's toes were curled under quite unnaturally

Ed in front of Irish cottage where his mother grew up

and I was shocked to discover it was because he wore his older brothers' hand-me-down shoes whether they fit or not. When the three Duggan boys outgrew their shoes, their mother mailed them to Ireland to be worn by cousins. As shoes were passed down, you just wore them, whether they were your size or not.

The home in Brooklyn where the Duggan boys grew up was quite modest, in a middle-class neighborhood. They didn't have a car. They took the subway to school and work. Ed's father worked at the courthouse before he retired, and, speaking of the courthouse, I'll never forget attending Ed's first jury trial. He was so excited to be going to court and I wanted to be there to support him. Unfortunately, I had never been to court before and didn't know what was appropriate to wear. I wore the dress pictured here. It was definitely not appropriate for a court room. Ed was mortified.

Thank God for his great sense of humor! We later laughed about my first "court appearance," but at the time, it was definitely a distraction. Another outstanding trait of Ed was his love of the written word. He read everything. He'd come over when we didn't have money to go out and he'd read to me. He was amazingly well-read.

As a boy, Ed had polio and spent time in a wheelchair. His parents didn't think he would live, but he recovered and seemed strong and healthy until he got t-cell lymphoblastic leukemia in his mid-30s. We'd been married less than a decade when he died at St.

Vincent's in Manhattan in the Village (that hospital is no longer there).

I moved into the hospital room with him and made things as good as I could for him. We knew so many young people. The doctors and nurses turned a blind eye to my large cooler that was kept stocked in the room so that I could offer a beer to his friends who came to visit. The treatments were awful. He lost his hair as he lost his health. Ed died on Christmas night. The last couple of hours, Ed told me, "I'm tired." His brother Gordon was there and got up to go home but I told him, "Gordon, if I were you, I'd stay." He was grateful to me for that because he was there when his brother died.

After Ed passed away, Bob and Miriam Meshel invited me to their house in New Jersey. It was a beautiful home on top of a mountain. As a joke, I pushed Bob into a closet and closed the door right in front of Miriam. I was a "Blonde Bombshell" and I had to live up to my reputation, after all. It sparked a good laugh!

The Meshels remained friends over the years, even after they moved to California. They came to visit once after I married Milton. They were the couple I mentioned who were sitting at our dining room table when I said something Milton didn't care for and he jumped up and ran to the phone upstairs and called me, so they couldn't hear the conversation. "It was an uncomfortable evening for us, to say the least," recalled Bob. "Iva's second husband was a rich wacko!" Miriam has since passed away and Bob and I have stayed in touch for years, catching up with phone calls and texts and promising that some day we would have another visit. It has been something I've anticipated happily.

Sadly, at about 2 p.m. on March 29, 2022, I got a phone call from my dear friend, Bob Meshel. His voice quite solemn, Bob told me that he was in the presence of his children and grandchildren and that this was his last call to me. He was going to be given an injection that day that would end his life, but before he left this earth, he wanted to call and tell me how much he loved me and had enjoyed our friendship. It was the saddest call I've ever received. Bob was my oldest friend. The memories we shared are now mine alone and I miss him … I miss knowing that he is just a phone call away. It is comforting to know that he had such loving family with him at the end. Bon voyage, Bob! Hopefully, I'll be seeing you at the next stop!

Nearly everyone remembers exactly where they were and what they were doing on 9/11, the day the Twin Towers fell. I was living at Windsor Place in Jacksonville preparing for a La Chaîne dinner. Liz Grenamyer was catering that night and when she saw me at the gas station on King Street, she ran out and grabbed me. "We're being attacked!" she shouted, pulling me into her place where people were all sitting and watching television and talking about the Twin Towers being hit by planes. All I could think about was the law offices where Ed worked on the 52nd Floor of the Twin Towers and how I would go to the club on the 52nd Floor at lunch time. I went home and spent the rest of that day in a fetal position. I learned later that Frank Loomis, one of the head partners in the firm, was late for work that day and missed the attack. I also heard that tugboats – probably the McAllister Brothers – got the admiralty lawyers (Ed's firm) to New Jersey that day. I remembered some great parties on the 52nd Floor … 9/11 brought back so many memories that I couldn't make myself go to the location where the Towers had been for a long while. There were too many spirits and memories there. Several years later, I went by cab to the memorial and spent solemn moments there.

I've always been sensitive to spirits and the spirit world. Ed's spirit came to me shortly after he passed away – I distinctly heard him say, "Iva." Daddy's spirit came to me at Windsor Place early in the morning as I laid on my bed in my room, thinking of him. We had buried him the day before. I must have been talking with him because Ivan came into my room and said, "Mom?" I also remember feeling unusual spirits and sensing a strange language being spoken occasionally when we lived in the Ortega house with Al Wells. Apparently, the ground where the house was built had previously been a burial place of the Timucua Indians. Yes, the spirits are still around me and sometimes I still feel an eerie rush of air that reminds me in a warm way of Ed or Daddy.

Know the rules well, so you can break them effectively.
~ Dalai Lama

5

BREAKING THE RULES

I broke one of my cardinal rules when I started dating Milton – never date (and certainly never marry) a man you've worked for. I look back and realize, though, if I hadn't broken the cardinal rule, I would never have given birth to Ivan, or known Jason and Francesca.

I first met Milton Ross when I went to work for Milross, his company. I was working the booth at a trade show for Milross, doing demonstrations of electrical/ mechanical products. Plastic was very big back then and Milross manufactured the liquor bottle caps for Jacquin's Liquor. They looked like crowns. I was also doing a magic card trick at the booth. He was married when I worked for him and that, also, was a major no-no for me – never date a married man. He later divorced his wife, and that's when we began to date.

Early on, Milton's wife, Caren, came to the trade show. He'd been talking about how beautiful she was and how she was an heir of Florsheim Shoes. Caren had dark hair and was attractive. He had met her on a skiing trip with her mother when she was 19. She was much younger than he, and he waited until she was in her early 20's to marry her. I knew Milton and Caren as a couple for a while. She was the mother of his children, Francesca and Jason.

Milton looked me up after he and Caren got divorced. We ran into one another at a trade show and he started calling me. Although I had an unlisted number, he had my answering service number and my address, as his company had mailed me a check when I worked for him. When he called and left a message, I always returned the call politely, but at a time when he probably wasn't in the office. He sent me postcards from all over the world for a year and kept asking me to meet him in Philadelphia for dinner. At the time, I had a line around the block and no desire to travel to Philly for a dinner date – my poor doorman. It was because New York men would put up with not sleeping with me for about two months and then they'd get tired and move on – so there was always a new group of men for the doorman to let in. So, finally, after a year of postcards and phone calls, Milton called and asked me to have dinner with him in New York. I'd been on a double date with somebody who knew Milton - the man owned Jacquin's. He lived in Philadelphia and was a friend of my date. I said I only knew one man from Philadelphia and his name was Milton Ivan Ross. He recognized his name and said he was a good man. That kind of validated Milton, so I told him I'd meet him at the restaurant. It was a nice restaurant on 3rd Avenue and Milton was quite gentlemanly – on his best behavior. He knew gourmet food and was an interesting conversationalist. He talked about being a self-made man who started his company in a garage. I noticed he hadn't planned the evening particularly well, which was kind of unusual, considering how long he had been pursuing me. I later found out that Milton rarely planned things out. He flew by the seat of his pants.

Milton and I dated for years after that first dinner. We traveled all over the world – to the islands and to Europe. Sometimes the children traveled with us. Once we were in a hotel in Paris that had a parrot in the lobby. Jason was 8 or 9 years old and he kept playing with the parrot. I told him to be careful because the parrot might bite him, but of course, he wasn't careful. He put his finger in the cage and the parrot took it in his claw. Jason thought he wanted to sit on his finger, but the parrot was just getting a good hold on his finger so he could bite him.

By the time Milton and I finally got married, his children and I knew one another well. We had been on many trips together and Francesca, especially, wanted a mother. I was glad to be that person for her. Milton enjoyed taking me to gala events but got jealous when the charity committees for fundraising events would ask me to help with the event or be on the board. He wanted to "show me of" but he didn't want me to have a brain in my head or actually be part of any of the organizations which he supported through his factory.

During the years we dated, Milton and Caren were fighting over the house and custody of the kids. Caren had a sister who lived in London and when she came to Philadelphia, I would be the one to take the children to the wife and the sister.

I really had nothing against Caren. Milton wanted nothing to do with her and I acted as sort of a buffer. What I eventually realized was that Caren had married Milton to get away from her domineering mother who was an alcoholic and used to beat her daughters with her high-heeled shoes. Caren jumped from the frying pan into the fire by marrying Milton. Suddenly, she had two children and had to deal with Milton, too. She was young and inexperienced and turned to drugs. Poor Caren. Their divorce was final, but they were still arguing over the settlement of the house and money – and what a house it was!

The Ross Estate was at 400 College Avenue, Haverford
(Recently listed for sale on Zillow for $4,900,000)

Caren was still living in the guest room at the house when Milton and I started dating, although I found out later that Milton had removed all her furniture and taken all of her clothing at that time – doing his best to make sure she came out of the marriage with nothing of value. I was not aware of his cruelty to Caren or anybody else for that matter. When we were together, he was as charming as he could be and we were with his fawning business associates, who would never say anything negative about him. He was a marvelous traveling companion and an exciting lover. The kids were at camp and I was trying to help Milton's mother,

Clare, one day in Center City when I noticed that some of the gorgeous clothes Caren had worn at society events were in Clare's closet, but it didn't register then. I was to learn later that both Milton's mother, Clare, and Caren's mother were troubled women.

Arson and Death

Milton dropped me off at his house one day and went to the factory. When we were dating, I often spent the weekend with him at his beautiful home, and this particular day, the kids were at camp and I thought I was there all alone. Never one to be idle, I ran upstairs to the master suite and got to work, cleaning the linen closet. I had filled a box with stuff and put it outside in the hallway when I heard something and opened the door. A blast of heat hit me in the face. The box of linen had been set on fire and flames were shooting up to the ceiling. I slammed the door and called the fire department. They asked "How will we know the house?" and I told them, with my usual calm, "It's the one with smoke coming out of the windows."

I found out later that Caren had set the fire in the library downstairs and also set fire to the box outside the master suite, knowing I was in there. When the firemen arrived, Caren was waiting at the end of the driveway and told them I had started the fire. She told them I was crazy and had a gun. The whole thing is so bizarre. The police actually knocked on the master suite door and I actually said, "Who is it?" Yep. I must have been a bit crazy, after all. They got me out of the master suite, down the stairs and outside and that's when I said, "Oh My God, I've got to go back in and get the babies!" Heidi, the Doberman, was in the billiard room nursing 7 or 8 puppies. I led the firemen back in and sure enough, Heidi was there, snarling at these big firemen wearing gas masks as I was down on the floor, counting puppies and putting them in a cardboard box. We got the puppies out through the basement and up through the kitchen. I put Heidi and the pups in the car in the garage.

Since Caren had accused me of starting the fire, the policemen came and put me in one patrol car and Caren in another. They asked me if I would take a lie detector test and I said, "Absolutely, yes!" Caren refused to take the lie detector test. Meanwhile, Milton went to the house and found Heidi and her pups safe

42

in the garage and black walls and fire damage in the library and master suite hallway. The police brought me home and we never filed charges against Caren. It was pretty obvious who set the fire. Since she was still Mrs. Ross and still living there, it was impossible to claim insurance on the fire. You can't set fire to your own home and be reimbursed.

A couple of weeks later, we drove up to the house and I felt a strange feeling – it was like a spirit - I knew Caren was there. I ran around the house looking for her. When I went into the upstairs study, it was dark. I touched her before I saw her. She was sprawled on the daybed – cold and stiff – rigamortis had set in. She had obviously died of a drug or alcohol overdose, as she had thrown up and the area was a mess. I felt numb. I called the police and they came right away. They were running up the stairs and I told them, "You don't have to hurry. She's gone." Milton came in and began taking the jewelry off of her body. He called her sister in London and said, in a monotone, "She's dead." She was taken out in a body bag and I did what came naturally to me … I cleaned up the mess before the help came. The police came back to the house and asked to see where Mrs. Ross had died. I told them I'd been trying to clean it up. "You what?" They asked! "Is that the vacuum you've been using?" They took it with them. Her mother hated Milton and accused him of murdering her. We didn't pick up the children for quite a while. Milton said the kids couldn't go to the funeral without him and he was not welcome there, so they had no closure. It was all over the newspaper that she had died. The children came home to a nightmare – black walls and melted Tupperware from the fire – and no more mother. They had not been close to Caren – Milton had controlled everything - but it was still shocking for them to lose her and not even be allowed to go to her funeral.

I was still Miss Cowford – naïvely in love with this powerful rich man. What happened to Caren was beyond anything I knew, growing up in Jacksonville. I didn't understand then that Milton was a sociopath.

No ability, no strength and force, no power of intellect or power of wealth, shall avail us, if we have not the root of right living in us.
~ Theodore Roosevelt

6

LIFESTYLES OF THE RICH & FAMOUS (SOCIOPATH)

Caveat: This chapter may be difficult for some to read, but it is all true.

When Milton and I got married, we had the ceremony in his gorgeous home. It was going to be just a small quiet wedding, but things snowballed out of control. All the people in Philadelphia wanted to give us parties before we were married – as well as the people we knew in New York, London and Paris.

My marriage to Milton Ivan Ross was a package deal: Francesca was 10 and Jason was 11. There was also one female Doberman named Heidi and her offspring, one male Doberman named Harold, as well as one black female cat named Elizabeth and two hermit crabs.

Life in the suburbs was different.

One day I'm on the sidewalks of Manhattan and the next I'm chasing a grocery cart down a hill. Let me explain – as I lifted the last bag of groceries out of the cart, the cart started on down the hill with me in pursuit. The cart picked up speed as I lost speed and it stopped in the middle of a four-lane highway. A truck driver looked at me as though I had been waiting on the side of the road to push it out at the right moment.

There are no incinerators in Haverford. One icy night, when Milton was still at the office and the help had all departed (the Help is another series of stories and will be taken up later), I decided I'd better do something about the garbage situation, so I dressed stylishly and warmly and loaded some of the mountain of garbage in the wheel barrel. As I was slipping and sliding down the drive, I began to laugh at myself. At the end of the drive is a slight incline and I began to slide on the ice with a bag of garbage in my arms.

Mail in Haverford is different, too. There are no mailboxes in the warm lobby. You must retrieve your mail from the box near the road. In times of bad weather, this is no easy task. Two mornings in a row I slipped getting our mail from the box. Two mornings in a row, the same man drove by in the same car and saw me in a mad embrace (death grip) with the mail box.

Another thing you do in the suburbs is shake the trees. We had a lot of snow this past winter and one evening it rained on top of everything else. The temperature was low and it formed ice on all our beautiful trees. This can do a lot of damage and I didn't know this. About 11 p.m., Milton started to get dressed. I asked him where he was going, to which he replied he was going out to shake the trees. Not to be outdone, I began putting on layers of clothes and joined him in this new activity.

Another thing you do in Haverford is plow your drive after it snows. Milton was on a business trip and I was in New York for a few days of bookings. The children and our housekeeper, Lee, were snowed in. But no fear, for I knew we had a service that plowed when it snowed. Our son, Jason, however, was unaware of our arrangement. When they phoned to ask about plowing the drive, Jason, knowing the cost and also knowing he only had $1.50, told them no. So, on arriving home, or at the entrance to the drive I should say, I found a great wall of white stuff blocking my path. Being from Florida originally and unaccustomed to snow, I was sure that if I backed up and picked up a little speed, I could push that snow aside. You have to realize that the snow at this point was about three feet high. It was like running into a brick wall. I retreated to our nearest neighbor's home, which was plowed, parked the car, took out my luggage and began to walk through their property, climbing over the fence and through the bushes. Fortunately, the children had left on the house lights and this was my beacon.

Self-service garages ... I was aware of garages with self-service islands and full-service islands. I usually selected the latter of the two. I was meeting Milton and delivering some equipment to him one evening. Our rendezvous was a Sunoco Station at the Bellemont Exit off Route 76. When I arrived, Milton had been delayed, so I thought I would make use of my time and fill up. Several cars pulled out and when the attendant finished with the car on my left, I leaned out the window and asked him to please fill my car up with unleaded. His response was "Fill it up yourself lady, this station is all self-service." Indeed, it was. After further observation, I saw a big self-service sign and another next to it that said, "Pay before you pump." Yes, it's a whole new world in suburbia.

And speaking of cars, for a year after we were married, I drove a Bricklin. Never heard of it? There's a good reason for that. It's like the Delorean – an extinct automobile that lasted for a very short time – and for a good reason – the Bricklin was a piece of junk! It came in only one color – Orange – and was supposed to be the sportscar of the future. Hah! A friend of ours, Malcolm Bricklin, a Canadian and the designer of the car, gave me a Bricklin to drive for a year. It was a two-seater made of fiberglass. I had gone to the factory in Canada on a tour

1975 Bricklin

and ended up with the car. It was definitely not the car to be driving in the snow in the suburbs of Philadelphia! I was on my way to Didi Borghese's home – about an 8-minute drive – and ended up in a ditch by the side of the road. A policeman got me out of the ditch and asked me where I was trying to go. He told me to follow him and he'd take me there. Unfortunately, I ended up in the same ditch a couple of days later, and the same policeman got me out and helped me get to the Borghese home again.

The Bricklin was jazzy looking and sometimes it attracted crowds because of it's design, but the doors were crazy. They opened from the bottom out and sometimes they wouldn't open at all. I'd have to crawl out the back of this monster. When I took it to New York, it stopped traffic. It was definitely different, but I was glad when I had another vehicle to drive.

Finally, after a year of driving the Bricklin, Milton made a big deal in front of my parents about buying me a brand new nine-passenger station wagon. After everyone had gone home, he handed me the bill for the car and told me to pay it. Some gift!

And traveling from suburbia to other places was also a whole new world after I married Milton. Ah yes, traveling with Milton was many things … different, for one. Fun, exciting and exhausting for another.

Several of the trips I had the privilege of taking after I married Milton had to do with the Y.P.O. (Young President's Organization). Milton was a member and I was his wife, so that qualified me for the many exciting trips the Y.P.O. planned for their membership. I remember going to several lovely destinations and I was known among the other wives as the lady who availed herself of all the services offered at every swanky hotel – the massage, the spa, the complimentary beauty treatment, the free tours of local attractions, the free cocktails and appetizers, etc. etc. etc. When someone wanted to know what was available at whatever resort we visited, they would look at each other and say, "Ask Iva." Y.P.O. was "top shelf" wherever we went. I think we were in Lucerne, Switzerland on this trip when we got white jackets.

Sometimes Milton went on the YPO trips and sometimes I went alone. As to traveling with Milton, I never knew what to expect. For instance, one evening I had been instructed to meet him at the airport. We were flying to London on business. I came running up to collect my ticket. A little late and out of breath, I gave my name and other pertinent information to the nice young man. Correct name, but the designation had been changed. You must realize this is normal for Milton. England at 5 p.m. had been changed to Germany at 7 p.m. I said fine

One trip where all YPO members got special jackets

… just give me the tickets and I will run. The young man gave me a somewhat bewildered look and said, "But don't you care if it's London or Dusseldorf? One is in Germany and the other is in England." I said no, relieved him of the tickets and left a somewhat confused airline person behind. The place was really not that important and I'd been to both. Milton was the fun … not the city.

As to religion, Milton and the children were born and raised Jewish. I was raised protestant, in the Methodist faith. My first husband was Catholic but I never converted. It was an ecumenical background for sure, but nothing to really prepare me for life in a Jewish home. I took private lessons from a local rabbi to help me learn what my duties were as a mother in a Jewish home. I even learned the traditional prayers in Hebrew. I ended up knowing as much or more about the Jewish religion than most of the Jewish people I've met.

One Seder before we were married, Milton and I were doing all the buying, preparing, etc., with the children for the Seder - a wonderful sharing and learning experience. It was a long day and much preparation. At 9 p.m., we were just setting the table for the meal. I was very tired and Milton walked in and said we had to reset the table in the main dining room because this table was glass and the children could see us passing the matza. Seeing my haggard look, he said it was okay and we'd eat in this room. I said no, we would reset and do it correctly, which we did. I thought we were all ready when Milton entered and asked where was "E's" cup. I thought oh no, he's invited someone else to dinner and didn't tell me. I look up and said "E" who? He laughed and explained that Elijah was a spirit, so I said, "In that case, "E" can come, sit down and let's begin."

Another difference is the food. One day I was cleaning out the refrigerator and saw two jars of pickles. That's silly, I thought, and a waste of space. I'll put them in one jar, which I did. The next day at lunch, I heard a cry from the table. It was Milton. He wanted to know who put the pickles in the matza ball soup! I don't know much about matza balls … they look like pickles to me. So you see, there was much for me to learn about Jewish food as well.

I kept a journal for a while during those years and here are a few of my entries:

February 8, 1979

Mama came to take care of the children while Milton and I were in Jamaica for a long weekend. Jason and Francesca will be fitted for braces this year so they seem to be aware of teeth lately. While Mama as here, Jason asked her if she ever had braces. She said no. Jason looked up at her and complimented Mama on her straight teeth. She thanked him. Mama has false teeth.

Jason is 11 years old and recently we have had many conversations on growing up, sex, the birds and the bees (to coin an old phrase). I was explaining about puberty and a few days after our conversation, Jason confused puberty with poverty. I explained that poverty came after puberty.

May 11, 1979

Sometimes I feel like we are living in a house we cannot afford, seeking out company and acquaintances of people who do not really care about us, maintaining a social life with men and women with whom the only thing we have in common is that the association can lead to future business.

There's hardly a parent alive who does not have some regrets and painful memories of failure. Children are infinitely complex, and we cannot be perfect parents any more than we can be perfect human beings. The pressures of living are often enormous and I get tired and irritated. I am influenced by my physical body and emotions, which sometimes prevent me from saying the right things and being the model parent I should. I don't always handle Francesca and Jason as unemotionally as I wish I had. I care too much. It's common to look back a year or two later and see how wrong I was in the way I approached a problem.

Lord, you know my inadequacies – they are many. You know my weaknesses, not only in parenting but in every area of my life. I do the best I can, but it's not good enough. Make up for the things I do wrong and in that delicate moment when Francesca and Jason stand at the crossroads of right and wrong, satisfy the needs I have not satisfied. Wrap your great arms around them and draw them close to you.

I love you enough to bug you about where you go, with whom and what time you will be getting home.

I loved you enough to stand over you for two hours while you cleaned your bedroom, a job that would take me fifteen minutes.

I loved you enough to let you both see anger, disappointment, disgust and tears in my eyes.

I loved you enough not to make excuses for your lack of respect or bad manners.

I loved you enough to ignore "what every other mother" did.

I loved you enough to let you fall, hurt, stumble and fail.

I loved you enough to let you assume the responsibility for your actions at nine, eleven or thirteen.

I love you enough to accept you for what you are, not what I want you to be.

Most of all, I loved you enough to say no when you hated me for it. That's the hardest thing of all.

June 1979

St. Vincent's Hospital

When does the transition come? The changing of power. The transferring

51

of responsibility and duty. Did you take your nap, Mama? Where are my glasses? What did you say? Where's my flight number and time of the plane? Last year, 1978, we celebrated Thanksgiving at our home. I prepared the turkey and Mama helped set the table. I feel very protective of Mama and Daddy. As children grow strong and independent, the mother becomes more vulnerable and childlike. All the years she bathed, dressed, fed, advised, disciplined, ordered, care for … now the tables have turned. I bathed and patted dry the body that once house me. I spoon-fed the lips that kissed my hurts. Now I comb her hair, arrange the covers, accompany her to the bathroom. She seems so frail. (Mama was ill quite often, and I always went home to get her through her most recent illness).

Wednesday, July 25, 1979

6:15 a.m.

Instead of this period in our marriage being one of happiness, it's been a painful experience to realize that someone I've loved and given to without reservation lives with so much fear of his wife. It's as though your capacity for love and trust has been retarded somewhere long ago. The absence of what I would consider the normal feelings of concern, protection and providing for me in case of some tragedy is painful for me to see and hear. Your reply to Marvin's question concerning some provisions for me – what do I get in return – how sad, Milton. I keep asking myself, "What have I done to this man?" You are so very sad, my darling, and I feel frustration and a helplessness.

It's been two long painful years to accomplish so little. The things that come so easily and naturally to other men don't come so naturally to my Milton. It's depressing to see the distance yet to go. I feel so sad and sorry for you and me. I'm unable to quiet your fears by love and deeds and loyalty. Your fear is a destructive cancer to our marriage. It is far more painful and killing to the spirit and our love than Ed's cancer of the body. I see no end. You cannot overcome I and I cannot do it for you.

> *Teach me to die, hold onto my hand.*
> *I have so many questions – things I don't understand.*
> *Teach me to die – give all you can give.*

If you'll teach me of dying, I will teach you to live.
I know that it isn't easy – seeing me this way,
And it hurts to watch me lying there day after day.
Trade your fear of parting for the faith that knows no pain.
Don't be afraid to say goodbye. I know we'll meet again.

*****

Discipline – Latin – training that develops self-control, character, orderliness and efficiency.

Milton and me – Christmas 1979

Christmas 1979

 Forgetting those things which are behind and reaching forth unto those things which are before, I press toward the mark for the prize of the high calling of God in Christ Jesus.— Philippians 3:13, 14

 If God had not sent us His son, to be born in Bethlehem, we would be forever without hope or joy. God came to man because man could not go to God. And the angel said, "Fear not, for, behold I bring you good tidings of great joy, which shall be to all people, for unto us is born this day in the City of David a savior which is Christ the Lord. — Luke 2:10, 11

Saturday, February 9, 1980 (Ivan's birthday)

7 a.m. Some contractions began and by 10 a.m. I was having contractions every three to four minutes. Mama, Daddy and I departed for Booth Hospital on City Line Avenue and arrived around 11 a.m. We had phoned Milton from the house and he was aware of our progress. My mother was a nervous wreck as I approached the desk. A midwife asked if she could help us and I said yes, I thought I was going to have a baby. I told her the contractions were three to four minutes apart. She asked mother and me to have a seat in the solarium; that there were a few ladies ahead of me. I could tell that Mama was upset, to say the least, with the casual manner and was muttering that at St. Vincent's in Jacksonville I would already be in a bed or wheelchair.

After they examined me, I phoned Milton but told him to take his time and finish his lunch. He arrived an hour or so later with camera equipment in tow. I labored until 9 p.m. when it was decided a C section was in order. I had walked the halls with Milton, taken a hot shower for an hour, and done deep breathing. With great difficulty and two more enlargements to the cervix, Ivan Robert Ross was born about 10:10 p.m. with Milton taking incredible movies and stills of the entire procedure. I thank God each day that Dr. John Franklin, Mabel Forde and Linda Bishop were on duty that night. They have the intelligence combined with compassion and sensitivity that I needed for support and encouragement. Robyn Winders, Judy Politzer and Dr. Tarampi, anesthetist, were also assisting in the operation. Milton stayed through the night and it was wonderful to know he was there. Mama and Daddy stayed a while and then returned to the house to be with Francesca and Jason. Francesca received a pair of gold and ruby earrings from her brother, Ivan Robert, and Jason received a watch.

On Sunday, Mama, Daddy, Francesca and Jason came to visit Ivan Robert and me. Monday, Milton's mother, Clare Ross, and his brother, Gene, came to visit and Sue and Mickey Sternberg dropped by. I must say that the next week was difficult. I felt the worst, physically, that I have ever felt in my entire life!

Back to my journal:

Friday, February 15, 1980

I came home. Milton surprised Ivan and me with a chauffeur driven limousine ride home. He had yellow roses inside (we had the same at our wedding) and we stopped off at our friend, Didi Borguese's house on the way home. The only terrible thing about my hospital stay was that Milton and I disagreed on having Ivan circumcised. It is medically quite unnecessary and I was against it. Milton wanted it done and on Thursday, February 14, 1980 at 11 a.m., and with me holding his little hands, Ivan was circumcised. It was awful and I was angry and depressed at seeing our son in pain. I thought of the many parents with sick or dying children and I understood that strong bond which

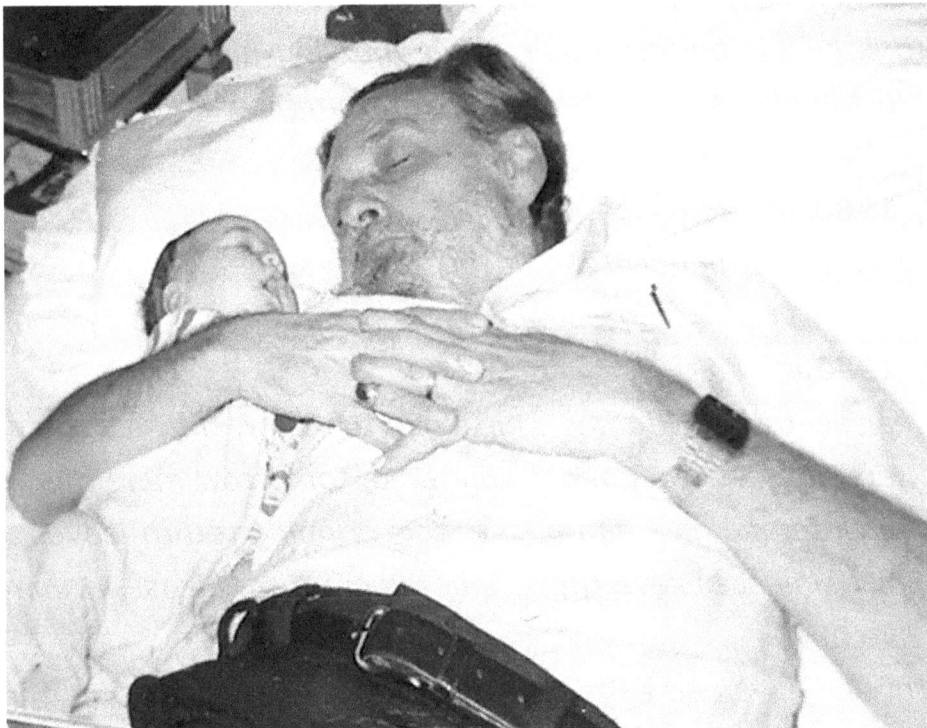

Ivan and Daddy ... passed out

I had never experienced prior to Ivan's birth – that bond of protection or kill to protect instinct that I had often heard of. I thought that if anything should ever happen to Ivan, I could not bear the pain and I felt more of an understanding of that part of life which was beyond my experience and comprehension. I love him so much and cannot imagine life without this little one. It's only been a week and it is as though he has always been with us. All the corny cliches I've ever heard are quite true about him making my life complete.

A couple of funny things that happened in the hospital were on the occasion when I had the strength to shuffle across the hall to the shower, someone would say, "Oh, you're his mother." Ivan was a giant among babies – a 10-pound baby among 5 and 6 pounders, and we had the dubious distinction of being the oldest mother and father, also the grayest daddy. I also know what the Greeks mean by "the evil eye." I'm so happy that I'm afraid something terrible will happen and it will end.

Monday, February 25, 1980

Ivan Robert is now sleeping three hours at a time. Better than two hours. He also took off his button today. I was nursing him and he had a dark bloody object in his hand – it was the scab from his navel.

March 4, 1980

I must be getting stronger. Ivan doesn't seem so heavy.

April 10, 1980

A child near death I saw today – his smile too slow, his face too gray. His gaze not here but far away, and I wondered, tomorrow mine this way?

I hold Ivan close and give him a kiss – his grinning return leaves a feeling of bliss. So, I almost believe there is nothing amiss. Please let him always stay just like this.

He's warm and alive and eager to smile. All I ask is to keep him just for a while.

Who is to stay and who is to go? Until the last moment, who is to know? There's no rhyme or reason but this must be so. But I'm screaming inside, never Ivan, never – no!

I was thinking the other day … two and a half years ago I had no children *and now I have three. My life has changed considerably.*

The big joke about Mama is when she and Daddy came up to help out with Ivan, she brought her exercise records. She hasn't used or needed them, nor has she had the time for a newspaper since Ivan Robert's arrival. Daddy lost five pounds in one week just going up and down the stairs.

I was so sore the first week, it hurt to sneeze. Daddy and Mama were lifesavers.

During those first months after Ivan was born, Milton was insistent that we maintain some sort of a social schedule. When I left Ivan with my parents, they would have everything they needed from me (including milk collected by breast pump) for the baby until my return. One night, Milton and I attended a beautiful oriental party where I wore my special and opulent oriental robe from Hong Kong – one of the few things from those luxurious days that I still own. Daddy was babysitting Ivan. He got thirsty and opened the refrigerator and had a glass of milk (not knowing that it was my breast milk!)

As Ivan became a toddler, Francesca and Jason and I enjoyed playing with him, but Milton was rarely there to join us.

In October of 1980, after seeing me with Ivan, my mother-in-law Clare Ross did a complete 180 – from hating me and judging me at every opportunity, she decided I was not so bad after all and actually had a party for me! It was black tie at an elegant hotel in Philadelphia and she gave me a diamond bracelet.

May 5, 1982

Today Ivan stood on the handles in the kitchen to reach a bottle. Of course, loosening the handle in the process. I cried. It seems just a few years ago that Jason and Francesca did the same.

Milton is a human being with whom I have lived for four years. Yet it is as though we never have time to get to know one another. He trusts no one – it's so sad and I feel helpless and unable to break through. More than anything, I grieve over what we never say.

*Note: It doesn't matter how much money someone has … what matters is how generous that someone is … and how responsible with the money. Something happened when I took Ivan to the doctor for his first checkup – it was quite revealing about the "real" Milton Ross. The doctor asked if my husband was well and seemed strangely interested in Milton's health. When I pursued his line of questioning, he admitted that he had not been paid. What?! Here was my rich husband, the proud father with the chauffeur driven limousine there to bring home his wife and child, and he had not paid the doctor? I was embarrassed and immediately wrote the doctor a check from my personal account. I was learning, little by little, that Milton did not pay his bills.

Attending "The Extraodinary Evening of Oriental Opulence" at the International House

"The Help" and other stories...

One of our past housekeepers, Ingaborg, had said at the time of her interview that she loved children and animals. This was good, because we had both. She stated that she loved to cook and was a gourmet. I asked her to prepare escargot – giving her two cans of snails. A few minutes later, I received a buzz on the intercom. A whispering voice informed me that the cans

Francesca, Ivan, me and Jason - 1981

had been opened and the snails were all black. I reassured her that they were supposed to be and that she should continue with the preparation. Jason said she probably considered herself a gourmet because she had a gourmet cookbook. She only lasted a few months. I think the dogs, especially our puppy Harold, and the children finally got to her. She wore all white – white shoes, white stockings and white dress. Harold was constantly tearing holes in her stockings. One day, she was running for the kitchen door and slipped and rolled in some of Harold's droppings. This was one of the last straws. She called constantly to anyone for anything. This was pretty funny, because you have to realize that Herbert, her husband, was deaf (I had suspicions that he pierced his own eardrums after living with her for a time).

Lee spoke only Japanese and Carmina spoke only Spanish. But this did not stop the non-stop chatter that went on from morning to night. Ingaborg departed with a nervous twitch and was 20 pounds lighter. Jason told her that was great and she should lose 50 more. This was one of her complaints. We ate only fresh vegetables and fruit – no sugar or sweets except for special occasions when I baked.

Ingaborg and Herbert were Germans. I hired them while Milton was away on a trip. They didn't know he was Jewish until they met him. I noticed that Herbert would be grumpy early in the day and happier later. It finally dawned on me that he was a drunk. Ingaborg cooked and cleaned and Herbert was the house man.

I had a nursing baby and two older children. Milton was on a business trip and Daddy had come to visit as well. Herbert was rude to my father more than once and I told him to pack his things and get out. He went to the bar and got a drink and came out into the entrance hall where I was – drinking and ranting and raving. He said he wasn't leaving. I called 911. When the one policeman arrived he seemed to sympathize with Herbert, I asked him, "If I were your wife, would you leave me in this situation?" He ordered them out. They were packing and they wanted money and I told them to go to the factory and pick up their checks. I found out that Milton paid all of the household help on the factory payroll, which was illegal. He also drew with-holding from employees but kept it instead of giving it to the government. I remember one night, two men came to the house from the IRS and Francesca told them her parents weren't home.

Then there was Carmenia from South America. She wanted to learn English and was going to class while she was there. She worked as a housekeeper. Lee – another housekeeper - was jealous of her going to school – they would fight like crazy, although neither one of them spoke the other one's language. Lee said that Carmenia had had an affair with Prince Marco Borghese, our neighbor – I don't know if that was true.

Marco did leave his wife, Didi, when his mistress was pregnant with his first biological child. Didi couldn't have children, so they had adopted Fernando – who was Ivan's age. Didi told me one day that her husband didn't love her anymore. He had a pregnant mistress living in a beautiful apartment on Rittenhouse Square –very exclusive. I met her on a train one time. She was nice – young, tall and slender – years later, they married and she had other children. She later died of cancer.

Prince Marco Borghese was at my house a lot – at that time I was cooking and had a Cappuccino machine. He said the house where he was living in Haverford wasn't as large as the servants' home in Italy. He was a great cook and a good friend. I really adored him. His wife, Didi, was also a good friend. I loved her. Marco was easy-going and Didi was more high-maintenance. Her family was from Greece. They met in Europe and when he came to the United States, he looked her up. He was working for an Italian car company when he first came here. Didi was short, busty, dark haired -attractive – but when we would double-date, she'd get so annoyed because the Maitre de would put Marco and me together. Milton was prematurely grey with a thick head of white hair. He was nice looking and always nicely dressed. He spent a small fortune on his clothes – all custom made at Saville Row in London. He had five tuxedoes and 200 cashmere sweaters. He was a clothes horse and he

Prince Marco Borghese and his wife, Didi

liked dressing me, too. I figured it out years later, he got attention because of me – so he really showed me off like a new car.

He bought me an antique gold band. Pretty – not flashy. He bought me some jewelry like a Rolex watch, but he really enjoyed buying me clothes more than jewelry – Christian Dior – Hermes, etc.

On one trip to Paris, Milton came to our hotel room with a Hermes purse as a gift – it was beautiful, crocodile with an H for Hermes. He told me to wear it because we were going to dinner with his partner in Paris. I was putting things in it – compact, lipstick, etc., and he said, "Be careful – don't put so much in it." There I was again ... little Miss Cowford – don't spend $9,000 on a purse – put the cash in it! I later came to understand that I was a trophy wife. We would take empty suitcases to Europe and come back with them filled with clothes. I enjoyed designing my own jewelry and modeled a gold necklace I had designed that Marco had made while in China on a business trip.

Milton spent money like it was water. I suggested to him one day that we should put $100,000 in a shoebox and hide it in the closet. He just laughed and said, "Don't worry about money. I'll make more."

We had a six-car garage with a full bathroom and the policemen would drive their cars into it and drink coffee.

We had a four-room kitchen with four stoves and a walk-in freezer.

Milton at one time had a belt business – bullet belts – very popular at a time, but he went out of business. The leather belts were striking with bullets imbedded in them – and there were hundreds of bullet belts in the garage. I told Milton we needed to have a garage sale with the children.

I kept up with my modeling career but limited it – and kept a separate bank account. Once, Milton borrowed $200,000 from me. I made him sign an IOU. Joan Crawford did that with her husband, the Pepsi executive, and collected from the estate because of it. I got to write it off as bad debt with my income tax.

Milton left later on a business trip. I was nursing Ivan – it was winter and snowing outside – and I woke up freezing. Milton had left a cut-off notice on my nightstand. Who does that? I called the factory. They hated him at the office. I was told once not to sign a prenuptial agreement with Milton and I never did. I was young, healthy, still modeling and had a good savings account and no children, but I loved Milton and so I married him. I loved him so totally – we were the public picture of perfection – pretty wife and children, but there was nothing perfect about our lives. Milton was hated at his factory because he neglected to take care of his people, and Daddy eventually became one of his people, as he put him on the payroll. When Daddy was diagnosed with cancer, I was concerned about his health insurance and I talked with Milton about it. He said he'd put Daddy on the payroll, which I thought he should have done long ago, as half of his family was on the payroll already. Daddy had health insurance through the factory, which I made sure was paid up during the time he was alive. After he died, I found out there was no insurance at the factory. Milton truly did not take care of his people – including me. But, in high society, Milton wanted his image to be perfect, and somehow, he was able to maintain that image – at least for a while.

We had friends, Robert and Miriam, over for dinner one night and I joked that our house was the annex to the nuthouse that was right down the road. Milton got furious. He excused himself from the table and went upstairs and buzzed me on the intercom – telling me to ring a bell for the servants and finish the dinner.

Milton's mother, Clare Ross, was the monster-in-law from hell. She hated me and threatened that if I married her son, she's stand up and come yelling forward. She said I was a Shiksa (a non-Jew). We had a private tutor at home for the kids – Hebrew school.

We had planned a small wedding – rabbi and minister – but there had been so many lavish parties for us that the wedding and reception were huge. I did all the cooking from the appetizers to dessert. Mainline society came to the wedding. I

had been cooking and freezing for weeks. That wedding took on a life of its own. Daddy walked me down the aisle.

Of course, a house like we lived in needed many servants. I read the book Kids and Cash –to Francesca and Jason and suggested they learn to earn some money. Francesca asked, "Why don't you just give us allowance? Go to New York and model and make money and come back." I suggested that they could eliminate the middle-man – me – and babysit or shovel snow. Jason got the shovel and came back with $50 cash. The next day, the two of them were fighting over the shovel. They had to put half in the bank account and save half. Several months later, Francesca was talking to Jason. She wanted to buy a record. She said, "Let's see, I have to work so many hours in order to buy the record." It thrilled me. She got it. When I first lived there, they never made their beds. Francesca said why should I make my bed? I'll have a housekeeper to do that." I told her that she might or she might not. They learned to make their beds and hang up their clothes.

Another money-making scheme worked well. The Merrion Cricket Club was right down the road from our home and parking was at a premium when they had an event. We had ten acres for parking. The kids made a sign – Park Here for $10. We had at least 100 cars, so the kids made a bunch of money – all cash. I let them keep half and put half in the bank. The gardeners, of course, went ballistic, as the cars had parked on the lawn – or the grounds, as Milton called it.

Ivan was an adored and adorable child. I saw a chimpanzee on the Johnny Carson Tonight Show and got ahold of the agent and had them bring the chimp to Haverford to the house. It was a big deal – for Ivan's 2nd birthday! People heard that we had the chimpanzee and called, begging to be invited to the party!

John, the Irish gardener, was a drunk. He was so sweet – daddy called him Dull Normal. When I would go to New York for the day, I would give John the money to get a haircut and a shave. He was Milton's size so I picked out a suit and tie from Milton's wardrobe for him to wear and he became a chauffeur for the day. Milton didn't know it. John was helping me get Ivan ready one day and he put Ivan's shoes on the wrong feet. Ivan looked like a duck when he walked. We went to the 21 Club in New York, and I took John and Ivan and Daddy in. The Maitre de was kind of looking at John strangely. He looked like he didn't fit in but Ivan adored him. They were giving John the look and I talked to the manager. I said, "He's my chauffeur but he's also a bodyguard for my son. He doesn't look like it, but he could kill you with his bare hands." He looked at him differently after that.

John had MS and lost control of his bowels occasionally. He didn't share that with me right off the bat. We had more than one gardener and we had a tractor to cut the lawn – ten acres – so I knew nothing about John's bowel problems until he told me.

We had two Haitian women housekeepers – very superstitious. Their walls had to be painted red – their beds had to be placed in a certain direction. They were big women who believed in Voodoo. They weren't the best but they were good. Got them through an agency. The Anenbergs were our neighbors – and they asked, "Where did you find Theresa?" I told them, "God sent her. She showed up with a nun."

Milton wanted to put up a big front – the beautiful young wife and happy family – but he was not able to maintain it at home. He was not at all courteous to our help. He saw them as less than he was. He was also selfish and self-centered. He told his children that business was the most important thing in life – not family. He told Jason he had no talent. Ivan weighed ten pounds and I was nursing him 24 hours a day. By the time I got finished, I was exhausted. Milton complained loudly. He said, "I gained a son, but I lost my wife." He was insanely jealous of the baby and wanted to claim me as his own. It was not about love – it was about power. I later understood that he was a sociopath and that is what a sociopath does. At the time, his forcing himself on me was legal because I was his wife, but since then, that type of non-consensual sex has been ruled illegal.

In the meantime, as I said, everything looked beautiful on the surface. We had a formal family photo done on Daddy's 60th Birthday at the German American Club in Jacksonville, where Daddy was President. It was a black tie dinner, with a big band, dancing and drinks – a great party!

Back to the help, Christina came from Poland. She showed up and wanted to work in my home cleaning and cooking. She fell in love with Ivan. She cooked Polish dishes. She was over here on a passport for tourists and then things went

We had the chimpanzee for Ivan's 2nd birthday party!

terribly wrong in her country and her parents told her it wasn't safe to come back to Poland and that she should stay in this country. The papers ran out and she was illegal here. She just showed up at my door. She was there more than a year. I loved Christina. I brought her to Florida in the summer. I'd rent a beachfront house in Ponte Vedra, bring the children and Christina – take them all to the club for swimming. Christina was only 17 or 18 years old and terrified that the Polish police were hiding in every bush. I hired an attorney at my expense and tried to straighten things out legally for her.

Also, when I went to New York, I'd take Christina and the kids and we'd stay at Frank Loomis's palatial apartment. Frank was a beloved friend who worked at the same firm as Ed, my first husband. Frank and Ed and I had been a threesome – wild and crazy. We rented a house in the Hamptons in the summer and called ourselves the three musketeers. Frank was even taller than Ed and the three of us were quite a sight. Once, coming back from a party, the two of them picked

The image of a happy family ... Not!

me up and put me in one of those canvas mail carts the post office uses. They started pushing me down the sidewalk and it was fun until they let it go. We were on a hill and it was 2 or 3 in the morning as I rolled down the hill in that cart – completely out of control. They started chasing me downhill as I approached an intersection and caught up with me just in time. I wish I had a video of that night. Frank was crazy – fun – a drinker – and his apartment in New York was great – much better than staying in a hotel.

Frank had a snake for a pet and he fed him live rats and mice. He also had a debagged skunk in that nice apartment in New York. The doormen could have written their own book about Frank. For instance, one day the snake wasn't hungry, so Frank released the mice into the elevator and sent it down to the lobby. The doors opened and the doorman knew where the mice had come from. He called Frank and told him to come get his mice.

Frank was a very handsome attorney from Atlanta, Georgia. He had a girlfriend, Susie, who was an airline stewardess. She was supposed to go to Europe on a flight but it was cancelled. She grabbed a cab and got back to his apartment but Frank was not alone. That must have been quite a scene.

Frank cleaned up his act when the children and I visited. He usually went and stayed at a girlfriend's apartment for the three or four days we were there. Christina watched the children and I went to the theatre in the evenings or out to

66

L-R Back: Grandpa Herbert, Wife, Milton, Aunt Susan, Uncle Louis, Aunt Dot
LR-Middle Row: Cousin James, Sue, Mom & Dad, Ivan, me
LR- Sitting – Cousin Iva Sue, Jason and Francesca

dinner with friends. During the day, we took them to the zoo or museums.

Theresa Padraglia was with the nuns who lived at San Rafael Retreat House. When the gardeners left, the nuns would come over to swim. Sister Rose played the guitar. They liked to drink, so I sent over a case of wine when they invited us over to dinner. One night, there was a priest dressed in a long robe at the Retreat. Ivan was just a toddler at the time and I could see him giving the priest the twice over. The man had on a dress and a beard – that confused Ivan. He waited until there was a lull in the conversation and then asked the priest, in a piping voice, "Do you have a vagina?" I quickly distracted Ivan.

Sister Rosita, one of the nuns, brought Theresa over to the house. She was from Peru. Sister Rosita introduced her and said this was her biological sister and

Ivan and me ... looking happy.

she was on vacation and wanted to stay for one year. I didn't know at the time that Theresa was wealthy and had several homes in Peru. She couldn't get anything, including her money, from her country for that year, though, and she needed to work somewhere, so I hired her.

One day, I drove Theresa to the train station in Philadelphia because she was going to Washington for the weekend as a guest of the Peruvian Council. They were having a black-tie event and here was this Philadelphia reporter focusing on me and it was really my housekeeper having an exciting weekend. She had some magnificent jewelry – diamonds and broaches – and was dressed up to go to Washington. She was the best housekeeper I ever had. She knew how to run the house because she did it in her country. She was fantastic. We became friends and she came back to visit after she finished working for me.

As a model, which I continued to do for many years, I was always known as a good girl and I stayed a good girl despite the bad reputation of models. I can honestly say that I never did anything I couldn't send home. That's not saying I didn't love to take chances. I remember I once rode the electric bull in a restaurant in Texas. It was not an easy ride. I told the operator of the bull, "I'm a mother of three – make me look good." He did.

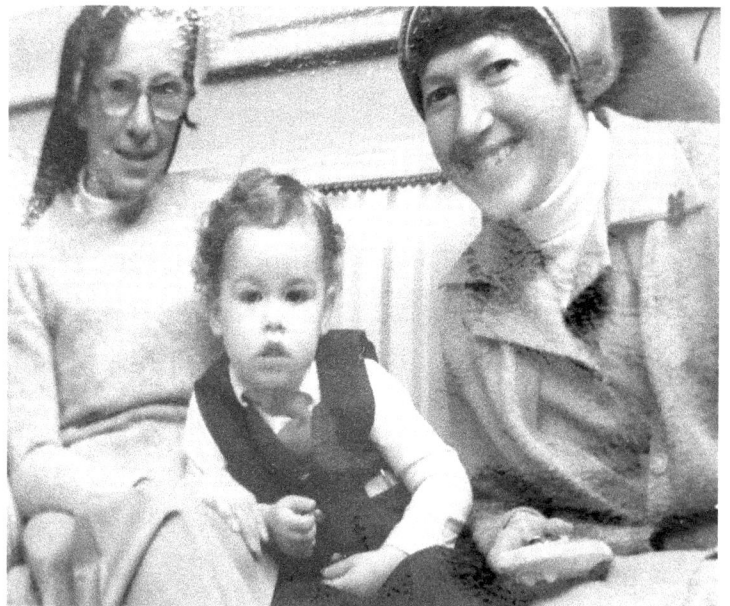
Nuns next door

My bone clings to my skin and my flesh,
And I have escaped only by the skin of my teeth.
~ Job 19:20

7

BACK IN JACKSONVILLE

I ran away from Philadelphia, escaping the marriage and the Ross Estate. General George Patton couldn't have planned my escape any better. I knew that this – getting away - was the most dangerous part of someone leaving a relationship. By that time, Milton and I had gone to marriage counseling with the same psychiatrist who had seen Caren, his first wife. In fact, when we went to the psychiatrist together, she looked firmly at Milton and said, "Milton, where have I heard this before?" Later, when I met with her alone, the psychiatrist explained to me that Milton was a sociopath – definition: A person with a personality disorder manifesting itself in extreme antisocial attitudes and behavior and a lack of conscience. Milton was charming and completely deceptive when he wanted to be – but he truly did not care about anyone but himself. Even after going to the psychiatrist, he showed no sign of changing. That's when I knew I had to get away from him.

I began planning my escape weeks before we left. I wasn't sure whether Jason or Francesca would want to come with us and I couldn't take a chance on them telling Milton, so I decided not to tell them we were going. If they chose to join us later, I would welcome them with open arms, but for now, I had to think of my own safety and that of Ivan. I made sure all the servants were off on the day the movers came and took what was mine (furniture Daddy had made, Ivan's belongings, my clothing and jewelry, etc.). The movers were enroute to Jacksonville by the time Aunt Dot, her husband, Uncle Carl, and Ivan were dropped off at Maureen and Brian Harrison's estate nearby. Maureen and Brian have remained good friends over the years. Recently, when I told Maureen I was

71

writing my memoir, she remembered the drama of that day we escaped. "Iva left with her bodyguard in case Milton reacted badly. She was, as always, beautifully dressed. She came back to our house just an hour or so after she had dropped off her son and her aunt. I knew she was meeting Milton at a Five-star restaurant and I asked her if she had eaten dinner before breaking the news to Milton. I couldn't believe she hadn't even eaten dinner. I think I gave her some milk toast to eat, as we'd already eaten."

I had arranged to meet Milton at a restaurant in town and had hired a big plain-clothes policeman to sit at the bar and keep an eye on things in case trouble erupted. I was waiting for Milton when he came in and joined me at the table. I confronted him, asking him if things were going to change. "Absolutely not," he replied. "Everything will remain exactly as is." I got up to leave and he tried to physically stop me. The police officer detained him while I rushed out and got in the car.

I drove to the Harrison's estate and picked up Ivan, Uncle Carl and Aunt Dot and we headed for Jacksonville. I didn't want to stop until we got home. My nine-passenger station wagon was loaded down with the four of us, two dogs (Sebastian and a stray mutt we had adopted) and all our luggage. When we stopped at a gas station in Maryland, I was so nervous that I mistook two policemen for gas station attendants and asked them to "fill it up." While I was busy changing Ivan's diapers in the backseat, they quickly accommodated me and gassed up the car. I thanked them and drove off without paying. It took a few minutes of driving down the road for it to register that I had not paid and that they were police officers in dark uniforms, not attendants. I turned around and went back, apologized, and paid for the gas they'd pumped.

We drove straight through to the beach house in Ponte Vedra that I had rented without Milton's knowledge. We stayed there for a month. Milton, of course, had gone ballistic and was calling everybody to find out where we were, but even when he did find out, he didn't come down, thank God. Instead, he sent Jason to me in shorts, sandals and a t-shirt to persuade me to come back. Jason was 16 by that time, and he turned the tables on his father – he decided to stay with us. He told me that everything was so calm and normal, he didn't want to go back. I said, "Jason, I love you and I will give you food and shelter and send you to school, but

Ivan and Jason

there will be no trips to the islands or any other luxuries."

Milton would call and talk to Jason for hours, offering him money and threatening not to send his car to him unless he drove it back home. Jason was not swayed. He wanted to go to the Bolles School and I sold some of my jewelry to pay for him to go. In the meantime, Francesca stayed with Milton. She had absolutely no parental supervision and, as a young teen, was going wild, having parties and loving the freedom to do whatever she wanted to do. Sadly, she never came to me, although I wanted her to. Francesca graduated from the University of Philadelphia and then went to California and was living in Hollywood. She was so smart and beautiful, but like her mother, she died in her early 20s of a drug overdose. Jason took care of arrangements for her. I was devastated. She left an empty spot in my life when she died. She was my daughter and I loved her, just as I love Jason and Ivan. Jason and his wife, Natasha, now live in St. Louis, Missouri and are quite successful in the fashion industry. They have a son and a daughter, Oliver and Alexandra. I'm in regular contact with Jason and family and that makes me so happy.

I began divorce proceedings right away and it was obvious that Milton was going to drag it out for years, fighting over property rights and money, as he had tried to do with Caren … and

Alexandra, Natasha, Oliver and Jason

now, there were Ivan and Jason to consider as well. He didn't fight for custody of Ivan, but he was legally entitled to have visitation with him and I had no choice but to send Ivan to him occasionally.

Ivan was conflicted, needless to say, and when he was four, I began to take him to Dr. Maria Victoria Acosta-Rua, a child psychiatrist recommended to me by my mother, who had been Maria Victoria's receptionist when she first started practicing at St. Vincent's. Actually, Maria Victoria knew my parents long before she knew me, but through Ivan, we became friends, and have remained lifelong friends ever since then. She helped Ivan so much back in those days and I'll always be grateful to her.

Also, because of the power that money gave Milton, I told my attorney to take the money off the table and simply ask for child support for Ivan. "Are you crazy?" my attorney exclaimed, not believing that I could do that with someone as rich as Milton. But I wasn't crazy. I had a small nest-egg and some fabulous jewelry I could sell, and I knew I was capable of earning money … I knew Milton well enough to know that he would wield his money like a sword for years if I allowed it. Once the money was off the table, Milton was virtually powerless.

Milton soon had a girlfriend, of course, and she would often be at the house when Ivan came to visit. She was actually a nice woman and tried to keep Milton from saying bad things about me in front of Ivan. Jason later told me that he was grateful I never said anything bad about Milton to him. Common decency kept me from it, but that didn't phase Milton. Thanks to Maria Victoria, Ivan had a grasp on what to do and how to react when Milton talked trash about me.

As to child support, the amount he paid me for Ivan's support was just another jab at humiliation. He sent a check for $96.00 every week and it took me quite a while to understand that it might bounce. I started cashing it right away. He told me that the $96.00 was a symbol of the sexual position 69. It was his not-so-subtle way of saying "fuck you" every time he wrote that check.

We moved into Windsor Place with my mother and it wasn't long before Jason asked to live in the garage apartment. He was a typical teenager, so I allowed him to do that. The divorce was still going on and I soon discovered that my mother was listening in on my phone calls and opening my mail. It was shocking and for a while, I couldn't believe she was doing it, but it seemed like Milton and his attorney knew everything about what I was doing and who I was seeing – things they couldn't possibly know unless someone was telling them. Finally, my attorney suggested I tell my mother something that only she and I would know and then we would see if she was passing information to Milton. Sure enough, when I told her a totally made-up story about Ivan and I going to visit Theresa in Peru, Milton knew instantly about it. How could my mother be doing that to me? I couldn't believe it! I've never been so hurt.

Later, in talking to a counselor, I was told that my mother wanted to BE me ... she wanted to live the life of the rich and famous – live in that gorgeous home and have all that money. Unfortunately, Milton showed an entirely different side of himself to her. I'll never forget the day Ivan and I went to the courthouse for the final divorce hearing. We ran into my mother waiting to testify against me. There she was - her hair all teased up, wearing red patent-leather high-heeled boots and a tight dress. I was appalled and poor Ivan was one confused boy. She later went on trips with Milton and Ivan, always the devoted grandmother to Ivan. I was grateful for that devotion to my son, but not for her betrayal of me.

Windsor Place, Avondale, FL

I was in my thirties, had just escaped a horrible marriage, and was eager to start a new life, make new friends and get involved in the community. People thought of me as a rich New York model who had come back home to make a big splash in a small pond. I did make a splash, but I most certainly was not rich … I had just learned how to stretch my money as a model and how to make things appear big and special even when they were small.

At first, Mother was glad I had come home because she thought I would take care of her now that Daddy was gone, and that she and I would be constant companions. Always a people-pleaser, I did take her many places and bought her whatever I could afford to buy for her. She loved the idea of having a popular daughter and going to all the posh parties, etc., but I was in a different age group and didn't want to always take my mother along, especially after I started dating.

Mother was also jealous of my sister, Sue. When I came back and got to know Sue as an adult, I realized that our mother had painted her with a black brush – saying things about Sue that were not true – indicating that she was a liar and a thief. With no cell phones and me traveling, the only information I had was Mother's version of things. One night, I was attending a symphony party with a good friend named Johnny and we invited Sue to join us. I let her wear some of my jewels, an absolutely magnificent dress that was covered with pearls, and one of my mink coats. We were getting into a limousine Johnny had ordered and mother ran out of the house shouting, "You shouldn't let her wear that – she'll get something on it – she'll steal your jewelry!" She was jealous that she hadn't been invited and she didn't care who she hurt. Sue looked gorgeous in that heavily jeweled dress and she never forgot that evening. A man walked across the room to her and told her she looked absolutely beautiful and didn't even look at me! Sue loved that, and so did I!

I have truly enjoyed going out to fabulous affairs with friends and even by myself. When a friend commented that she could never eat out alone by herself in a restaurant like I did, I just laughed. "I'm not eating by myself," I told her. "I'm eating with myself." I was always comfortable with myself and didn't mind going places alone and traveling with myself.

I went to the Cummer Ball and many other society happenings and soon got to know a lot of people and got back into circulation. I've always enjoyed the social scene and, even though Jacksonville was not New York or Philadelphia, there was a lot going on and I wanted to be part of it! I soon became involved in the Jacksonville Symphony, the Museum of Contemporary Art, the Cummer Museum of Art & Gardens, the World Affairs Council, the Cancer Society, Hubbard House, the Heart Association's Red Rose Ball, and so many other organizations that were philanthropic and cultural. I remember learning how to conduct a board meeting from being on the Symphony Board with the big guys – Preston Haskell, Jim Winston, Jay Stein and others. They knew how to do it efficiently, and I observed them and used their methods when I was president of the MOCA Guild and other organizations. It began to be reminiscent of my days in Philadelphia society when I was asked to be on boards like the Philadelphia Ballet and West Park Hospital – and Milton was so jealous that he was asked to donate but not asked to participate.

Being an active member on the board of various non-profits and charities satisfied my philanthropic tendencies, as I was always taught, especially by Daddy, to give back as much and as often as I can. Also, as a board member of these prestigious organizations, I was invited to participate in so many events and galas that I might not have been able to afford had I been on the outside looking in. I was also privy to special fares for trips through organizations such as the Cummer Museum of Art & Gardens.

Ivan and me in Washington, D.C.

Ivan and I went to Washington, D.C. with a group from the Cummer Museum for a five-day trip in the mid to late 1980's.

We visited Senator Bill Nelson's home, enjoyed an elegant dinner at a beautiful restaurant, visited the Smithsonian Museum and took a tour of the White House. There were several local philanthropists on that trip, including one of my favorites ... Betsy Lovett! Sadly, she recently passed away. She was such a personality ... I always nicknamed her "Auntie Mame." I hired a limo and driver one evening and invited another Cummer board member and her daughter to ride with Ivan and me. To drive around the capitol at night when all of the monuments and buildings are illuminated was an overwhelming experience. The trip was absolutely flawless.

When Ivan was in the Nutcracker's party scene, I became an extremely active volunteer. The Nutcracker literally took a year out of my life. There was such a competition between mothers that it was ridiculous.

This Nutcracker rode around with me in my car for weeks as I tried to sell him to the highest bidder. He and I became close buddies before it was over.

I remember there was a beautiful red couch at a popular restaurant, Crawdaddy's, that Linda Crofton (DJ Arthur Crofton's wife) and I basically stole because we needed that couch for the party scene. Linda was the executive director of the whole event and one of the few paid people. We were on a tight budget and I was the most enthusiastic and determined volunteer. That couch was just perfect for the party scene. I had spoken to the manager at Crawdaddies about borrowing the couch and he hadn't exactly said yes or no, but when we got there with a pickup truck, the manager was out and the assistant manager believed us because we walked in with such confidence.

Linda grabbed one end and I grabbed the other and the two of us carted it out of the restaurant. Who does that in the middle of a busy Saturday night? When the Nutcracker was over, we returned the couch, no worse for the wear. We were always looking for ways to save money because there was no budget for the play.

Just as the Nutcracker is a Christmas tradition in Jacksonville and all over the country, the Larson family had a special Christmas tradition when I was growing up. Grandpa Larson, Daddy's Daddy, would cut down a big, beautiful fir tree on his property, wrap it in burlap, and send it to us by train. Whenever I see or smell burlap, or a fresh-cut tree, I remember going to the train station to pick up our Christmas tree. Daddy would haul it home and we'd decorate it together. Daddy always cooked the Christmas or Thanksgiving turkey, too. I thought all men were like my Daddy – able to do just about anything – but he had grown up from a very young age without a mother and had, by necessity, learned to do what needed to be done.

Another Jacksonville tradition is the annual hatching of the sea turtles as they come up on Jacksonville Beach. I've seen three turtle hatchings, and actually ridden in the Turtle Mobile, which is much like a golf cart. The Turtle Man is a private citizen who took it upon himself to go out around the laying time when they lay the eggs and mark the nests. People who live in Atlantic Beach know that there are no lights allowed because the little turtles go toward the moon after they're hatched and if they see street lights, they might go in the wrong direction. People who live on the ocean in Atlantic Beach sit in the dark with a glass of chardonnay watching the sand. When the turtles hatch it sounds like popcorn popping. They move out of the sand and start moving their flippers and go toward the light of the moon, heading toward the water. I rode with the Turtle man a couple of times in the early morning. He would figure out where the eggs were laid the night before and put an orange fence around the location – so children didn't dig there. One neighbor came out with me after hearing me talk about how miraculous the hatching is. She had religiously watched but never seen it. She ran into her house to go to the bathroom and when she came out, it was already over. The tiny turtles are in danger from the minute they're hatched. The seagulls will pick them up and eat them and even when they get to the water line, the fish might eat them. But enough of them survive to come back every year to the same beach to lay their eggs. It is a fascinating miracle.

Ivan was my miracle. His birthday was always a big deal. I'd joke with him, "Where would you like your mess this year?" It was usually held on a Sunday. I always had an open bar for the parents of the kids … it was only for one hour, so how expensive could it be? The dads started bringing their kids, along with the mothers. All of the kids from school came – word got around. One year, they had all these balloons left from a cotillion the night before at Timuquana. Hundreds of balloons! After Ivan's birthday party got underway and we had the cake and presents behind us, I opened up that room full of balloons and they flew out on the lawn toward the river. The kids went ballistic, chasing balloons and popping them! It was such a joyful day! The gardeners must have hated me on Monday morning, though.

Ivan was attending Riverside Presbyterian Day School Kindergarten in 1984 when the following little article was written up about him in the school newsletter:

Kid of the Week

This week our Kid of the Week is Ivan Robert Ross, son of Iva Ross and grandson of Mrs. Bert Larson. Ivan is four years old and his birthday is February 9, 1980.

We are so pleased that Ivan has joined our Sunday School since moving back to Jacksonville last year. He is in the 4-and 5-year-old Kindergarten class and attends regularly. His teacher, Mrs. Carolyn Hurt, says that Ivan is a real pleasure to teach, always well behaved and anxious to learn.

Ivan is like most 4- year-old boys. He is in gymnastics classes and has his own little set of golf clubs that he practices with. But besides sports activities, Ivan is a bit different. He is already enrolled in the Denise Carol Modeling Agency and can be seen often in ads for May Cohens and other stores in Jacksonville. His big eyes and beautiful curly hair are easily recognizable.

Ivan attends the Riverside Presbyterian Day School Kindergarten and especially loves the crafts.

Ivan is just one of many special boys and girls here at Riverside Park but look for his picture in the Times Union!

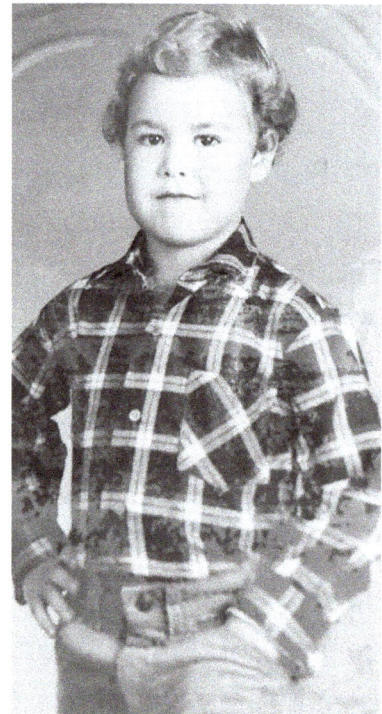

Not only was Ivan modeling for ads in the Florida Times Union, he could sometimes be seen on billboards. I remember seeing this one as we were traveling and coming to a skidding halt so that I could get out and take a photo of the billboard!

I was also still modeling for Midiri Model, Inc. in Philadelphia and was represented by Denise Carol in Jacksonville.

Ivan was about 7 or 8 when he decided he didn't want to be a model anymore. He said, "I've been working all my life and I'm not going to do it anymore." I thought to myself, "he'll feel different when he finds out what a paper route pays." His interests turned to art and literature and he wrote several short stories that were enjoyed by all, and he eventually returned to modeling, along with several other pursuits such as being a disc jockey and an amateur magician.

People here in Jacksonville were really impressed with the fact that I had been a New York Model and still did modeling occasionally. They didn't know exactly what to make of me, especially when I was able to bring special guests to Ivan's school – magicians like Walter Zany Blaney and the Palace Guards from London. When the Queen's guards came to Jacksonville, I entertained them. All the women were throwing themselves at them. They were just 19 and 20 year old kids who came here and got to ride in a limousine. A friend of mine was connected to the royal family and I ended up taking the guards under my wing. They went to St. Mark's School at my invitation, and they met the kids. I knew of them because I had spent time in London. They were just young sailors - actually, wearing an incredibly recognizable uniform.

Another time, I was involved with the Women's Board Art & Antique Show, with

The guards and me at St. Marks

NOVEMBER 27, 1978 $1.00

Here Comes SUPERMAN!!!

TIME

·NEW AMERICAN MANNERS·

Social Arbiter
Letitia Baldrige

THE BUSINESS LUNCH 1978

the theme "Diamonds and Diplomats." Letitia Baldrige, who had been Jackie Kennedy's Social Secretary and was the author of several books on proper decorum, was the guest of honor that year. She had run a Public Relations Firm and hired me way back when as a model for Sedgefield Do Nothing Jeans and I had been the main model in her Sedgefield campaign, representing the brand from Philadelphia to San Juan, Puerto Rico, but now, I was just a volunteer for the Women's Board and the ladies didn't believe me when I said I knew Letitia and I had been "Miss Sedgefield." I finally went to the hotel where it was "rumored" she was staying and when she saw me, she immediately said, "Oh, Iva, you are sitting at my table!" As I said, the people here in Jacksonville often didn't know what to do with me. It was a hoot!

Theresa/Homestays

My friend and former house-keeper, Theresa, came to Jacksonville and stayed with me. In Peru, she wanted her grandson to learn to speak English and have an American experience, so she told her daughter to let him come and live with me and go to school with Ivan to St. Marks Episcopal Day School. So, Theresa's daughter and grandson came to

IVA LARSON
THE WOMAN WHO PLAYS ROUGH ENOUGH TO WIN

Letitia designed the above button for me!

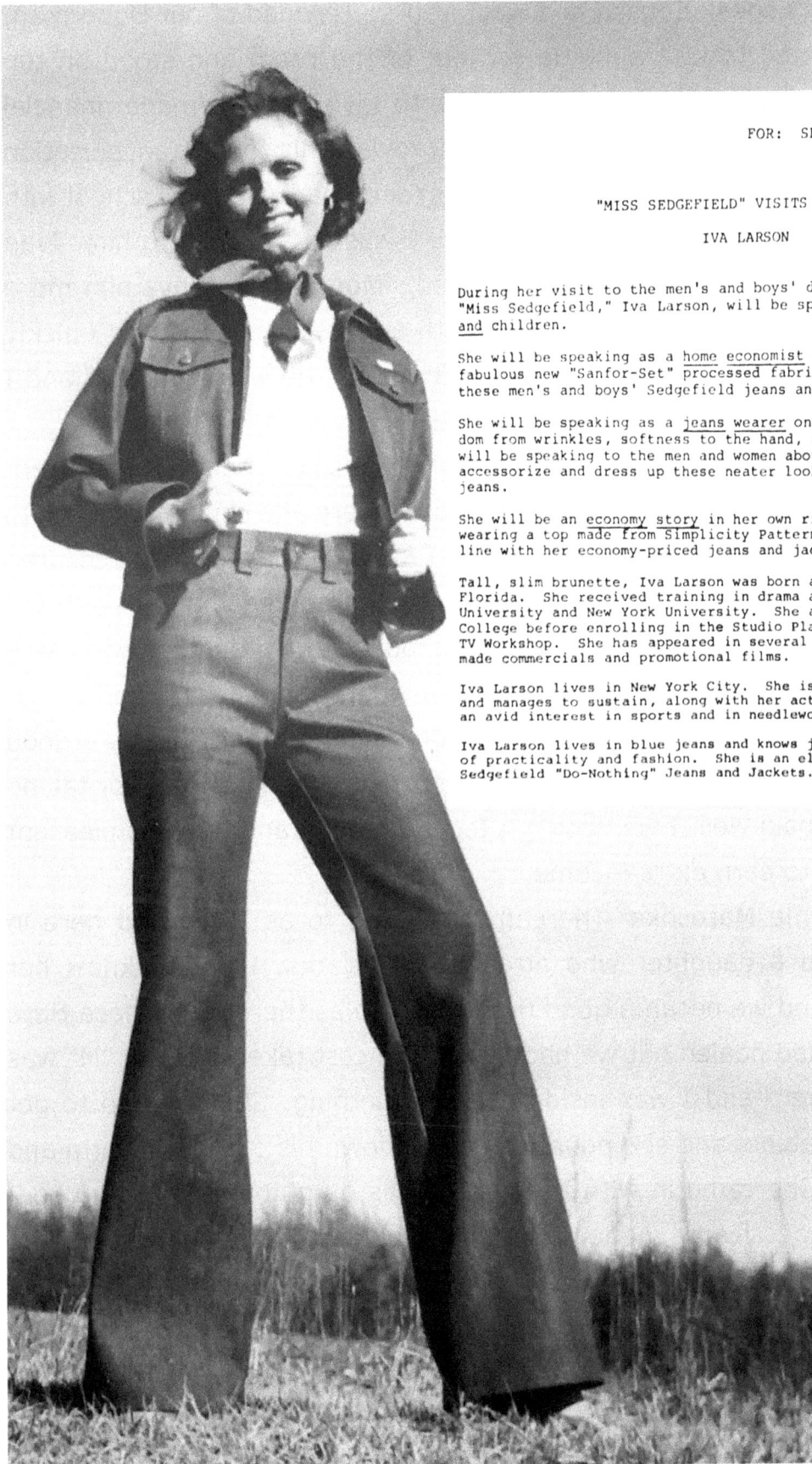

FOR: SEDGEFIELD DO-NOTHING JEANS ANI
JACKETS

"MISS SEDGEFIELD" VISITS THE STORE

IVA LARSON

During her visit to the men's and boys' departments of the store "Miss Sedgefield," Iva Larson, will be speaking to men, women, and children.

She will be speaking as a home economist on the subject of the fabulous new "Sanfor-Set" processed fabric which is used only for these men's and boys' Sedgefield jeans and jackets.

She will be speaking as a jeans wearer on the subject of fit, freedom from wrinkles, softness to the hand, and proper fading. She will be speaking to the men and women about fashion - how to accessorize and dress up these neater looking, wear-everywhere jeans.

She will be an economy story in her own right because she will be wearing a top made from Simplicity Pattern's Spring and Summer line with her economy-priced jeans and jacket.

Tall, slim brunette, Iva Larson was born and raised in Jacksonville, Florida. She received training in drama at both Jacksonville University and New York University. She also attended Jones Business College before enrolling in the Studio Playhouse and the M.T.I. TV Workshop. She has appeared in several industrial shows and has made commercials and promotional films.

Iva Larson lives in New York City. She is an accomplished musician, and manages to sustain, along with her acting and modeling careers, an avid interest in sports and in needlework.

Iva Larson lives in blue jeans and knows jeans from the viewpoints of practicality and fashion. She is an eloquent spokeswoman for Sedgefield "Do-Nothing" Jeans and Jackets.

Miss Sedgefield

83

Jacksonville. He didn't speak English and was, at first, terrified of our Doberman, Sable Ann, who wanted to kiss him. He ran out of the room and stood on top of the furniture in the study, but he later came to love her. We made financial arrangements and his mother paid $100 a week toward his food, transportation and what not. He was Ivan's age and lived with us for a year – going to school with Ivan. I broke down crying at the airport because I was so attached to him. Ivan had been an only child until he came. Ivan asked, "Mom, do you love him more than me?" Of course, I didn't … but he was cute and well-behaved and quickly learned English. That's the child I got through Theresa. She was my friend and I loved her. She later had a stroke and died in Peru.

I became involved in Homestays International because of Theresa's grandson. These were children who were getting their education here and couldn't go back to their country because of politics or whatever, so I found homes for these children to stay in until it was safe for them to go back. I ended up keeping a lot of them myself. Masa Hero was a little Japanese boy who looked like a buddha who came to live with us. He had a cast on his broken arm when he came. He had to eat what we were eating, so he lost weight. I had only healthy food. It was a good situation. I could be at home and take my child to school and get paid for taking in other children. It paid well. I was doing it for the money and it was a pleasant and convenient way to earn extra income.

My friend, "Madame Marushka" (hereafter referred to as "M") lived here in Jacksonville and had a daughter who attended St. Marks. I got to know her through the school and we became good friends. She was there when Masa Hero was there. His arm had healed but we hadn't had the cast taken off – so "M" was outside with Masa Hero and I was inside doing something. She came in to get salad oil out of the cabinet and she poured salad oil down his cast on his arm and pulled off the cast. She came in with the cast. I was dumbfounded. She joked, "Don't have any business cards made up yet." He was fine and happy to have the cast off.

"M" had a new Mercedes and she drove like the wind. We had Masa Hero and Ivan in her car one day going down to St. Augustine. I always told them to put on their seatbelts. Masa Hero wasn't buckled in when she missed a turn and without slowing down, went over the grass median and went to the next roadway. I turned to the back seat and Masa Hero's eyes were as big as saucers and he was in the process of frantically putting on his seatbelt. Never had to remind him again.

He had what he called a Hello Card and he could call whoever he wanted to call. He got a call from his parents when he'd been here for a month and they were correcting him that he should not use that card just to have long conversations with his friends in Japan. He was with me a year. It varied with each child. I had one who was not a joy at all. She was Japanese and very cold – never smiled – just wasn't happy. Of course, the communication was not easy. They all learned to speak English. They had to because they were going to school with Ivan and they were living in my household.

When Ivan was in 3rd grade at St. Marks, I took him to see the magician, David Copperfield. I had written a note to Copperfield and told him my son, Ivan, was entranced with magic. During his performance, David threw me a rose, and invited me up to the stage to help him with an illusion. Ivan and I were meeting my soon-to-be in-laws at the Timuquana Country Club after the performance. I was poised and well-dressed and I wasn't working with him, but everybody thought I was. He asked me questions which I answered. David Copperfield said, "We're on a date. Where are we?" I was thinking about dates in New York. "Oh, we're being picked up in a hansom cab at 19 East 76th Street and we're going to Tavern on the Green for dinner." That was all part of my life and it came naturally. There were tons of Jacksonville people attending that performance. When I finished talking to him, they uncovered the screen and all my answers were printed on the screen.

He pointed to his cheek and I kissed him there and Ivan and I left the stage. Later, we were invited backstage and Ivan became even more interested in magic.

I took Ivan on a Magic Cruise where magician Walter Zany Blaney was the main performer and again, we were singled out during his performances on shipboard.

**Walter Zany Blaney, Ivan and me
on Magic Cruise**

We kept in touch with Walter for years after that, and we actually got him to come to the school and perform for the kids.

Davy Crocket and the Go-Go Girl

Alfred Wells (columnist Judy Wells' brother) was a nice man who came from a wealthy Ortega family. Wells Road in Jacksonville is named after his family. Al had never been married and had lived at home with his parents most of his life. When I met him, I was new in town and didn't know anything except that he had a little apartment in Venetia. He had worked for First Guaranty Bank doing appraisals and owned a used car business. He seemed quite successful, but appearances can be deceiving. He thought he was marrying a rich model!

Al was an interesting man who wanted to date me exclusively with marriage in mind, but I wasn't interested in marriage. I told him, "Look, I just got out of a long relationship and an ugly marriage. I'm new in town and I don't want to limit myself to one person."

In those days, I would fly back and forth to New York just to get my hair done at Kenneth's. The airlines had special fares to fly up to New York and back for $30 or $40 in a day. I was dating several men at the time and one day they all wanted to pick me up at the Jacksonville airport. What a dilemma! I managed it, though. Al picked me up from my actual flight and took me home to Windsor Place. Then I took a cab back to the airport and the second gentleman picked me up. By the time I returned to the airport for the third time, the cab driver and the porter at the airport were getting suspicious, but I managed not to hurt anyone's feelings that day. I came back to Jacksonville as sort of a "Big Fish" in a small pond. I had been born here and gone off to New York to become a successful model. I was in no way a top fashion model, but I had done well enough, and I was still flying back to New York for the occasional modeling job. In my hometown of Jacksonville, I suddenly became an instant celebrity. It was fun!

Al did his best to monopolize all my time, but it didn't work in his favor. For instance, I was on the golf course at the Timucuana Country Club with Al one day and I felt a stabbing pain in my abdomen. He rushed me to the hospital. At first, the doctors thought it was my appendix, but it turned out to be pancreatitis. I was in the hospital for a couple of days and my room looked like a funeral parlor – there were so many flowers from so many men I'd dated. Al was not happy.

Al was sort of a Davy Crockett type – he had never traveled out of Florida and was not at all sophisticated. They called us Davy Crocket and the Go-Go Girl! Al never gave up and courted me relentlessly, going to La Chaîne parties and black tie events and being quite charming. We eventually did get married. I thought he was well-off and he thought I was rich. It was revealing when one day I walked into the Florida Yacht Club and was on the other side of a screen off the bar when I heard Al talking to the bartender, telling him, "I've married a rich wife. I'm going fishing!" Rich? Hah! I was just selling jewelry as fast as I could sell it and somehow, as always, making ends meet so that I appeared much more prosperous than I was.

We were married at the Timuquana Country Club on May 18, 1986. Big Al was best man for his son and Ivan was our ringbearer.

May 18, 1986

We were living in Ortega and Ivan was attending St. Marks Episcopal Day School in December of 1987 when a cat "somehow" snuck into our house and gave birth to eight kittens in our bedroom closet. Ivan was thrilled, of course, and the kittens were just as cute as they could be, but I have to say that our Christmas tree suffered ... I had to redecorate it about three times! It seemed like every couple of days, the tree and all of its ornaments and lights would start shaking and falling down due to a "kitten attack." We had kittens everywhere!

Finally, after giving away as many kittens as we could, I ran an ad in January of 1988 in the St. Marks weekly publication, as follows:

Ivan loved the kittens!

The ad worked. People clamored for the $500 kittens! We ended up keeping a couple of them, too. They were quite valuable.

Looking back, I think Al's family must have been thrilled when he married me, and they all loved Ivan. Ivan was the grandson they had never had. Al took Ivan fishing and got him a set of golf clubs just his size. He was really good to Ivan, often taking him camping. He loved Ivan, but other than my son, we shared few common interests. Al's sister, Judy, was nearer my age (Al was younger) and we had many of the same social interests. Judy and I would go out to gala affairs together and Al preferred to stay home in front of the television, watching sports. Al was so good with Ivan that I stayed with him as long as I could.

Al and I eventually went to a marriage counselor and it was all quite civilized. Our diverse interests

SMEDS "SCOOP" 1/15/88

S! Be sure to ask your children about the "Mask Man". This fantastic Theatreworks presentation was enjoyed by all our Level 1-6 children on Tuesday afternoon. Many thanks to the St. Mark's Parent's Council and especially Carol and Dan Bierce, our Super Friday chairmen, for providing the school with this wonderful opportunity.

Three kittens are available for adoption - $500.00 - 100% discount for SMEDS students. Please contact Ivan in Miss King's class if you are interested, 771-8070.

Choose a hat - any hat!!

Ivan with Al Wells

and the fact that we had really nothing in common made it clear that our divorce was a mutual thing. When I sat Ivan down and told him Al was moving out, his first question was, "Can I have his spot?" He meant Al's spot in my bed!

Artis Gilmore

I met basketball great Artis Gilmore at a Celebrity Chef's benefit for The Red Cross, where we were both volunteering. He was so friendly that I invited him over to the house to meet Ivan, who was a big basketball fan. That friendship led to Artis inviting Ivan to a special basketball camp.

**Ivan and Artis Gilmore
with another friend**

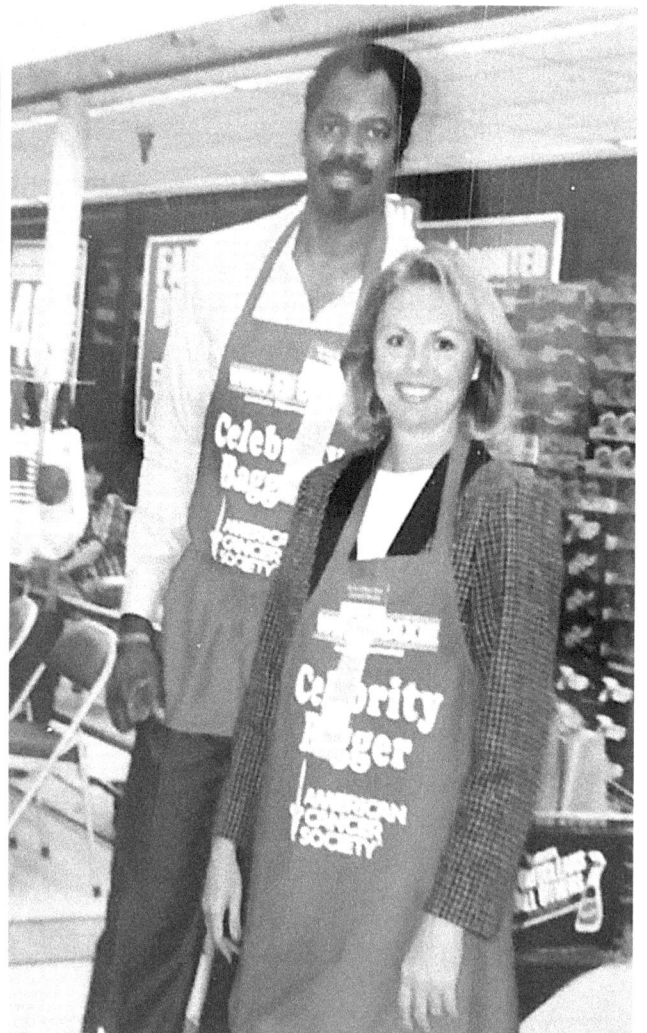

**Artis Gilmore and me,
"Celebrity Baggers"**

*A gourmet who thinks of calories
is like a tart who looks at her watch. "
~ James Beard*

8

LA CHAÎNE

I was one of the first women to be invited to join La Confrérie de la Chaîne des Rôtisseurs, an international gastronomic society originally founded in 1248 during the time of French King Louis IX (no … I wasn't present when it was founded!)

I was pursued by La Chaîne in Philadelphia. They heard about this crazy woman on the mainline who lived in a mansion and gave parties for 100 people and did all the cooking. I had a staff, of course, but I was in charge of the food and I loved it. I was flattered to be invited to join the society and joined in both New York and Philadelphia.

At the time, I was married to a jealous multi-millionaire, Milton Ross, who didn't understand why people wanted me to be in societies and on boards that he wasn't invited to join. La Chaîne enhanced my life enormously. It has a chapter in nearly every country and provides an instant "family." If you need a

Confrérie de la Chaîne des Rôtisseurs®
Bailliage de Jacksonville

IVA F. LARSON
BAILLI
COMMANDEUR

JACKSONVILLE, FLORIDA 32205
USA   TEL: (904) 304-9105

doctor or a lawyer or simply to meet a like-minded person who enjoys eating, drinking and having a good time – La Chaîne is the key that unlocks the door.

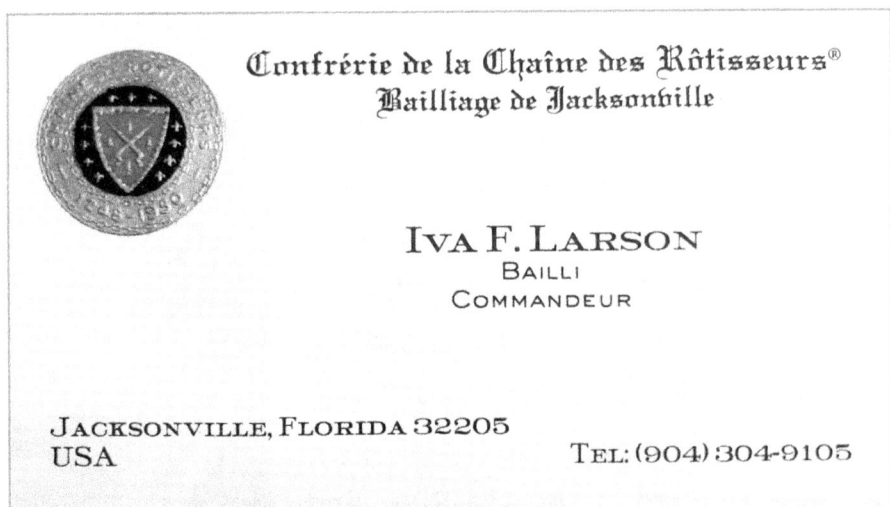

La Chaine event at Dwight's –
Dwight in the White Chef's Shirt

When members of the society visit Jacksonville, they would get in touch with me and I invite them to my home for drinks. I've met amazing people over the years. Chefs love to cook for members of La Chaîne and it can be done on a budget – always elegant, black tie. Dwight's Bistro on Penman Road in Jacksonville Beach and the chef at the Omni have each prepared meals for $95 apiece, including champagne and hors d'ouvres, with every course paired with a wine. Dwight Delude is an excellent chef and a dear friend of mine. He is deeply into La Chaîne.

La Chaîne has enriched my life immeasurably and when I established the first chapter of the society here in Jacksonville back in the late 1980's, I did my own thing. Because it was known as a predominantly male society – the men wore all the ribbons and the women did all the work – three of the five officers I chose for the Jacksonville chapter were women. I was Bailli Commandeur (President), Dr. Maria Victoria Acosta-Rua and Yvonne Corey were the other female officers. Plastic surgeon Bernie Kay

Dr. Gaston Acosta-Rua
and me (la Chaîne!)

and Restauranteur John Curington were the original male members. There are over 20,000 members worldwide and I now serve as Vice Chancelier-Argentier, Confrerie de la Chaîne des Rotisseurs as well as the founding President of the Jacksonville Branch.

Dr. Gaston Acosta-Rua, a neurosurgeon who was married to Dr. Maria Victoria Acosta-Rua, one of Jacksonville's first child psychiatrists, were two of my dearest friends. Maria Victoria lost Gaston to pancreatic cancer in 2003 and later wrote the memoir of their family, Las Memorias. Maria Victoria is still one of my dearest friends in the world, and both of us still miss the wonderful presence of Gaston. Gaston absolutely loved being a member of la Chaîne!

Gaston escaped from Cuba when Castro came in the 1960's and his gratitude for being an American citizen was in his heart for the rest of his life. As a gesture of that gratitude, Gaston and Maria Victoria had a huge "Pig party" every December – a Cuban tradition of roasting a whole pig and serving it to friends and family annually. It has become a tradition for the Acosta-Rua family in Jacksonville and continues to this day. I always wear my pig snout to the party. Here is a photo of my biographer, Susan D. Brandenburg, and me at an Acosta-Rua pig party in 2018.

The day I met Susan D. Brandenburg, I invited her to my home on Windsor Place for a glass of champagne before we headed for dinner at Orsay, a new French restaurant in Avondale. Susan had been assigned by a magazine to write a review on the new restaurant, which was "conveniently interesting," because she knew both the restaurant owner, Jonathan Insetta and his mother, Diane LaFond Insetta, quite well). As she settled in the living room after a short tour of my home, I decided to show her my skill at Sabrage, and came into the room brandishing a large

Susan and me at Pig Party-2018

knife. Susan always remembers it as a moment of pure terror for her. She had just met me that day at a MOCA Guild event and really didn't know this tall blonde woman who was waving a butcher knife just feet away from her! We've laughed about that moment many times since then and I've had the pleasure of sabering at several of her parties.

Champagne Sabrage (sabering): Legend has it that as Napoleon and his troops returned home victorious from battle, the townspeople greeted them with bottles of Champagne to show their appreciation and gratitude. Because the soldiers were on horseback, it was too difficult to put down the reins to pop the champagne cork, so they used their sabers, and Voila! The art of Sabrage was born! I learned how to perform this ancient art in order to save money. I used to pay $75 for someone to come and saber the champagne at La Chaîne dinner parties. The drama adds to the excitement of the meal, but I thought I could certainly do the sabering instead of paying someone. I didn't have a sword, but I had some large knives. I have since performed sabrage often at dinner parties and it always adds excitement. I've taught several people how to do it, but unfortunately, a few have ignored the rule of never imbibing champagne until after sabering. There have been times when the glass shattered instead of flying off the top of the bottle as it should, and a few people have suffered minor injuries, but all in all, sabering is a skill I've enjoyed using and teaching.

Since I founded the chapter here in Jacksonville, La Chaîne dinners have been featured in several Jacksonville publications.

In 1991, Jacksonville Today Magazine featured an article entitled "Exceptional Taste," by Lenore Greenstein, with the photo on the left.

1991 was a busy year for La Chaîne. Here's a portion of a feature story in the Jacksonville Register.

Photo featured in "Exceptional Taste"

The River Club was just one of the

La Chaine enjoys evening at Hidden Hills

HIDDEN HILLS - The Hidden Hill Country Club is having a busy April.

Prior to the opening of the Symphony Showhouses located at the community, the country club hosted a dinner for members of the Jacksonville Confrerie di la Chaine des Rotisseurs.

A lavish meal was prepared for Chaine members and guests by Jimmy Mahusay, executive chef de cuisine at Hidden Hills. Festivities got under way with a reception where guests were treated to Beluga-salmon-seruga serpentine, pate de canard and lavvash. A delicious escargot en croute l'alouse a la sauce Bearnaise was the appetizer that preceded the first course, filet de sole farci. The entree for the evening was escalopes de veau sur fond d'artichauts et champignons roses a la sauce Chambertin.

Wines served during the evening included J. Lohr "Riverstone" 1988 Chardonnay; Kenwood 1989 Sauvignon Blanc; Morgan 1988 Piont Noir; Leecocks "Rainwater" Medeira and Remy V.S.O.P Cognac

Host for the evening was Dame de la Chaine Yvonne B. Corey, manager of Hidden Hills Country Club.

Xavier and Carole Salinas, Jo Baker, Bruce and Irene Pearson

nd Lewis and Thomas Albright

Judy Wells and Ande Albright

Mel Jawitz, Marcia Coplan, Iva Wells and John Currington

many wonderful venues where La Chaîne dinners were held. In January of 1992, we celebrated the 5th Anniversary of my founding on the Jacksonville Chapter at the River Club. Although she is not pictured here, one of my favorite people, Betty Boyer, was inducted into La Chaîne that night. Her husband, Judge Tyree Boyer, also became a member. It was a sought-after membership in Jacksonville.

And, in 2009, one of my favorite la Chaîne parties of all time was held at the Acosta Rua Home on September 20 and an article was written by Carole Salinas, Vice Chargee de Presse for Gastronome Magazine, as follows:

La Chaine members toast fifth anniversary

The Confrerie de la Chaine des Rotisseurs, Bailliage de Jacksonville, held its annual induction dinner Jan. 25 at The River Club.

The black-tie event featured a menu that charter Chaine members will recall from the group's first dinner five years ago. That dinner was also held at the River Club. The menu was recreated in honor of the group's fifth anniversary.

Menu items included hors d'oeuvres of caviar, sushi, salmon and champagne, a frogs leg and escargot bisque, creme glaze fromage and a spectacular dessert.

Inducted into la Chaine were Thomas Albright, Audrey Baker, Carolyn Baker-Singleton, Elizabeth Boyer, Charles Holbrook Jr., David Nicoll, Bruce Pearson, and George Trotter.

The Chaine was founded in France in 12 by learning royal chefs but was disbanded when royalty fell out of favor. In 1950, the Chaine reorganized with chapters forming throughout the world. The Jacksonville chapter was founded in 1987, boasts 75 members and meets at least eight times a year at various restaurants to enjoy the best in food and wine.

Chaine Bailli is Bernard Kaye. Vice chancelier argentier is Joyce Kaye. Ira Larson Wells is vice consiseilli gastronomique.

Bruce and Irene Pearson, Wayne and Jo Singleton, Nacrio and Carole Salinas

Ber Bell and his Wife

On September 20, The Jacksonville Bailliage held its fall event at the elegant, Spanish-style home of Vice Chargee de Missionss Maria Victoria Acosta-Rua. We admired the paintings and other artwork in her home while sipping champagne and nibbling baby lamb chops that tasted as thought they were made in heaven.

Dinner began with barbecued wonton duck with Boursin and balsamic reduction. Beneath the shredded duckling was a base of tantalizing sweet potato. The accompanying wine was a fine Savignon Blanc by Morgan. The second offering was a medley of field greens with toasted pine nuts, Parmigiano-Reggiano, and aged white balsamic vinaigrette. A Chardonnay by Steele was the salad's ideal wine complement.

The entrée took center stage, and we enjoyed in silence perfectly grilled petite filet mgnon with lobster bearnaise, dauphine potatoes, and sauteed haricots verts. A Blu Franc, also by Steele, was an excellent choice with this course.

The grand finale was an aptly named "decadent" chocolate cake with a molten chocolate filling that wrapped itself around raspberry

coulis with caramel and fresh berries. A Seghesto Zinfandel enhanced this treat. After the meal, Bailli Iva Larson presented Vice Chargee de Missions Acosta-Rua with a Chaîne decante and thanked Executive Chef Charyl Clark of Heirlooms Bistro for an outstanding dinner. With this autumn affair, the Jacksonville Bailliage's new Chaîne season got off to a rousing start.

Western Barbecue or ...
God Forbid I Miss a Party!

I met Marilyn and Mal Kirpich in New Orleans at a la Chaîne event in 1988 and they later invited me to their Western Barbecue at the stables of their gorgeous Frank Lloyd Wright house in West Palm Beach. Of course I showed up! God forbid I miss a party! I learned later that Mal had been captured by the Germans during the holocaust and held in a concentration camp. No matter how wealthy he became, he still looked at each plate around the table to make sure no one had any more than he had.

Cowboy hat and silver boots

It's useless to hold a person to anything he says
while he's in love, drunk, or running for office.
~ Shirley MacLaine

9

PROMISE HER EVERYTHING AND GIVE HER NOTHING

My fourth (and final) marriage was to a man named Alvin Maynard Coplan. I nicknamed him "Promise her everything and give her nothing."

Coplan and I met at an event at Epping Forest. Ivy Prescott invited me to a monthly singles event there. He joked that when he walked in with me on his arm, the men galloped over ... he said it was like the running of the bulls at Pamplona! Ivy was a good friend – nothing more. He had beautiful blue eyes and white hair and a lot of money. I called him a "walker" – he would attend fundraising galas when a man was needed. Ivy was a lot of fun!

That night at Epping Forest, Coplan asked me to go to dinner with him. He also asked me what my favorite restaurants were. I later found out that he owned the Syrian-Lebanese Star Newspaper and would get free meals from restaurants in exchange for advertisements. Ivy said that Coplan was so tight that he squeezed a nickel until the buffalo farted!

When he was courting me, though, Coplan presented himself as a generous, loving man who wanted nothing more than to help me put Jason and Ivan through the best schools and give me a wonderful life. He truly had me fooled.

Over the years, my last name changed temporarily, but my passion for La Chaîne remained the same. In 1998,

March
Members of the Month
Alvin and Iva Coplan

The Coplans enjoy many of the Club's special events such as Gourmet Wine Dinners and member mixers. They always celebrate the holidays at the Club with their family and friends. Both Alvin and Iva are members of the elite Chaine des Rotisseurs dining society and encourage the group to select Epping Forest Yacht Club for exclusive dinners. The Coplans travel around the world and are always looking for new and exciting food and wine experiences. Thank you Iva and Al, for your support. Congratulations!

Alvin and Iva Coplan

Coplan and I were featured as Members of the Month at Epping Forest Yacht Club, identifying us as members of the elite Chaîne des Rotisseurs dining society and world travelers.

Back in the late 1980s, Coplan, Ivan and I went with my friends, Drs. Gaston and Maria Victoria Acosta-Rua, to Europe for the Vin Expo in Bordeaux. We flew from here to Paris, where Maria Victoria's sister, Guadalupe, was having an art show near the Louvre. I remember we were walking in front of the Louvre and ran into Bob and Carol Shircliff and their grandchildren – what a nice surprise that was!! We all went to see Guadalupe's art show together and enjoyed it immensely! Then Ivan went to visit Guadalupe's family for a while and we four took the train to

Paris with the Shircliffs, Acosta-Ruas, Ivan and Guadalupe

Bordeaux and then rented a car through Coplan's connection with the newspaper, pretending we were press. We visited the Vin Expo in Bordeaux and tasted wonderful wines and we went to a vineyard there and had a beautiful visit as "members of the press." The hostess treated us to good Spanish ham and seafood – a gourmet meal with fine wines.

Coplan and I were on the Amalfi Coast in Italy – a beautiful, two-lane road, but I saw very little of the scenery as I was holding on for dear life as he raced to our romantic hotel. I was feeling anything but romantic by the time we got there. Coplan never had a car he didn't crash. He was an insane driver. I had had enough and I told the concierge to get me some train tickets to Paris, which was our next destination. I was not going to ride in the rental car with Coplan again. When he heard that I was going by train, he had a fit, but he straightened right up and promised he'd drive carefully. I cancelled the train reservation and we had a decent drive to Paris.

He was always wheeling and dealing – a great salesman who promised to send the boys to the best schools but reneged on his promises after we got married. We moved to his beach house and I started decorating it. We had mirrored walls and chandeliers and silver – I love mirrored walls … they create light and space in a room.

Ivan and I went on several trips together without Coplan, which he didn't understand or tolerate well. In fact, once when we were gone, he jealously went through my chest of photograph albums and threw away or destroyed many of my precious photographic memories.

Later, when Ivan was older, we went on another Magic Cruise on Carnival Cruise Lines. The magicians gave him private lessons because they said he reminded them of themselves when they were young and interested in magic. Sometimes, the magicians came to Jacksonville and stayed with us and performed at St. Mark's School for Ivan and his classmates.

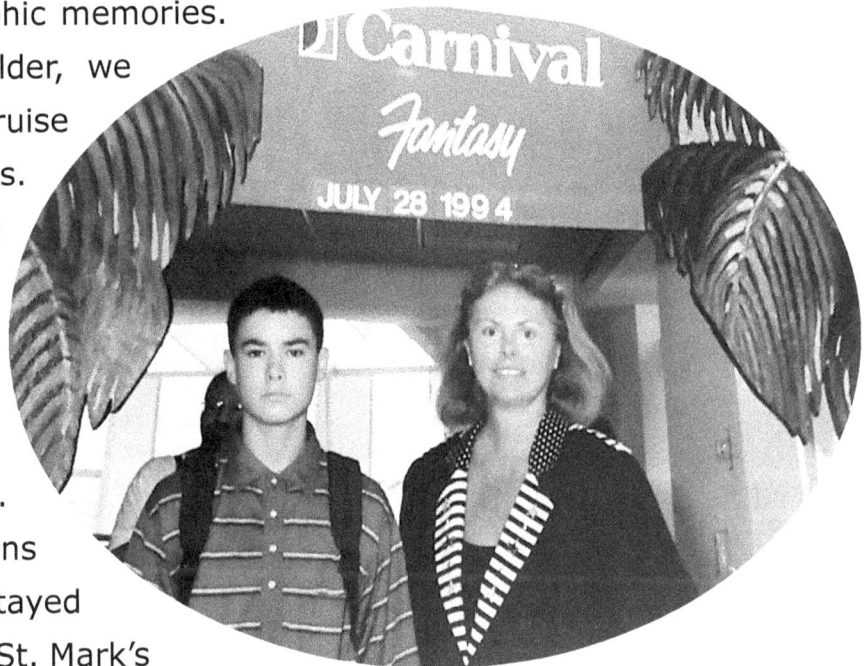

Like his mother, Ivan graduated a year early from high school. The last two years of high school, he attended Douglas Anderson. He was so talented in so many things … he made me proud!

Ivan was so ultra-talented and such a handsome young man that he became a celebrity at a young age. When he was just 16, he was already a well-known Disc Jockey who did his own music tapes and had a booming business. I took him on a business trip to Las Vegas one time when he was about that age, and by flashing my La Chaine card, got us a complimentary luxury suite at the hotel where we had reservations. We walked in and he said, "Wow Mom! This suite is bigger than

Ivan's graduation from DA

our condo at home!" He made good money and got more and more well known, and by 2001, when he was just 21 years old, he was traveling the world doing his promotion of PUMA.

Unfortunately, Coplan was insanely jealous of Ivan and every other person I spent time with other than him. One night, he completely lost his temper and attacked Ivan. Ivan ran to the police station and called me and when the police came, it was obvious there had been a brawl in the living room. Ivan and I didn't go back. We stayed at the Sea Turtle for a few nights and then he went to visit Milton and I floated around to the homes of friends while I was trying to sort out my life. Coplan began stalking me after I left him. He put a tracker on my car, broke the car window of friend where I was staying. Police said he wanted me to know it was done intentionally, as a brick was placed on the car. I went to a gated community in Ponte Vedra and he somehow got in there, too. He isolated me ... I couldn't even escape to my sister's house in Avondale.

Police came and gave me information on what to do:

- Take trash somewhere other than where you are living
- Don't take the same route home and be aware if someone is following you. If yes, go to police or fire station – do not go home.
- Put a bathmat on the floor where you come in – fluff it up when departing and upon entering, check for footprints.
- When out in public, always sit facing the door and if standing, keep your back to the wall.
- Get a P.O. Box – no mail delivered to your home.

As I got closer to the police department and police officers started to know me by name, I became curious about what types of situations besides mine that they ran into regularly. I saw Sheriff John Rutherford at a charity event and asked him if I could go on a ride-along sometime. He arranged one for me and after signing all kinds of waivers and disclaimers so that they could avoid liability if anything happened to me, I got to go out on a ride-along in a patrol car one night. We were in the Moncrief area of town at one point and the officers detained a hooker for questioning. While they were looking up her record, I talked with her and discovered that she, too, was a mother. We had a nice conversation – just two women talking. She was, after all, a human being, and so am I.

At another bad area of town that night, there was a shooting and the officers

ordered me to stay in the car. It suddenly occurred to me that I was the only one there who didn't have on a bullet-proof vest! Another interesting thing that happened that night … we knocked on the door of a house where a "domestic" had been reported and the officer told me that he could tell they'd been there before. How? There were marks on the wooden frame of the door that showed they had hit the doorframe with their sticks to get someone to answer their knock. It was a night I'll never forget.

I haven't been everywhere, but it's on my list.
~ Susan Sontag

10

WORLD TRAVELER

Cuna Indians

My travels began when I was 19 and working for Prudential and have continued all my life. The last big trip I took was to Costa Rica for Tony Acosta-Rua's wedding a few years back, but I'm going to chronicle as many of my fabulous foreign experiences as I can in this travel chapter.

I was doing a shoot in the Panama Canal Zone and I was talking to an American woman at the hotel swimming pool one day when she asked, "Have you visited the Cuna Indians on the San Blas Islands?" She insisted that I must visit them before I returned to New York. Always up to a new adventure, I listened to her advice. She connected me with a small airplane and off I flew to the San Blas Islands; the pilot, a Cuna Indian, a chicken and me. We flew over miles of jungle and then the pilot landed in a clearing of dirt and grass. "This plane is too big to go where you're going," he declared.

Hmm. That was pretty frightening, but I've never shied away from adventure, so I got into an even smaller

Panama jungle

plane that took me over even more jungle to a small island. We landed safely and soon, some Cuna Indians paddled out to pick me up in small wooden canoes. This was obviously before the cruise ships and tourists discovered the Cuna's and the beautiful molas they created.

We were on a tiny island with no access to fresh water. The Cuna's paddled over to the mainland every day for water. They were tiny people and they found me fascinating. There were always about a dozen of them following me around. I was a giant among them – fair and tall and friendly – they treated me like a queen. I loved their diet of bread and coconut ... they baked the most fantastic bread on their wood-fired ovens. I watched them sew their exquisite molas and learned to spot quality in both molas and people. They were quality people for sure.

I stayed with the Cunas for about three weeks ... barefoot, wearing a sarong and a straw hat, eating fish and bread and coconut. The men took me to other islands, where they shopped for supplies. The women weren't allowed the leave their island. I found the Cuna Indians to be warm and friendly and respectful. We spent a good deal of time smiling and laughing. They spoke Cuna and Spanish, neither of which I understood, but I knew that a smile and a thank you are the same in every language – and body language is so important to communication. They knew I respected them, and they returned that respect.

It was a great experience, even though there were absolutely no amenities ... I lived in a straw hut and there were no chocolate or roses on my pillow. It was one of the most pleasurable adventures I ever had.

In the world of the Cuna, daughters are valued over sons, the reason being that when they marry, the husband comes to live with the bride's family. There was a two-daughter family on my island and the father was such a difficult task master that they were having trouble finding a man to marry.

My hut in the Cuna Islands

106

Egypt

Two memories of Egypt come to mind:

Ed and I were once on a trip to Spain and I told him we were so close to Casablanca, we should go and see it. We rented a car in Cairo – a British Duchavo which looked like a prehistoric animal. It had a gearshift that looked like an umbrella handle and Ed was having car trouble and checking the engine on our way to Fez when two men in white sheets and turbans came from the side of the road. We were sure that we were going to captured by white slavers, but they helped get the car started for us and sent us on our

Francesca, me, and Jason – Egypt

way (no doubt talking incessantly about the tall blonde and her tall husband in the strange car). Later, in Casablanca, we could bask in the hotel pool and look up at the skiers in the mountains. We met an Italian oil baron at the hotel and he told Ed to get rid of our rental car and come with him. He knew the country. He did, and we went off with him, ending up our trip in Italy. Ed talked about that trip forever, saying it was such a joy, and so different from the trips he took while in the Navy. A little adventure never hurt anyone, right?

Then, a few years later, there I was ... in Istanbul! I couldn't believe I was in the land of the pyramids that I had read about so many years before in the book about the Seven Wonders of the World! The sounds and the smells were overwhelming – there was no way to be still and read a book in Istanbul. There were people kneeling on the sidewalk to pray, loud bazaars and the bustling marketplace – I wanted to see everything in Egypt. I lost my luggage on the way to Cairo. All I had was what I had on – a comfortable purple dress and brown boots. I shook the dress out every night and prayed I wouldn't get BO (body odor). I was searching for cream because my skin dried up in the climate. I remember, when I asked for some cream, the manager at one hotel told me he gave facials, but it turned out to be a ploy. He wanted to give me more than a facial. I got up and, pointing to my neck, I told him, in no uncertain terms, "In the U.S., a facial is from here up!"

The Egyptians were mad at me. I had no luggage for them to carry – therefore, no tips. My purple dress was beautiful – a rich, brilliant color – a dress from Paris – but it was all I had.

My future husband, Milton Ivan Ross, and I were dating at that time and his children, Jason and Francesca, joined me in Egypt on this trip (which I still remember fondly as my "purple dress trip").

I rode a camel while I was wearing that purple dress and that was one of the smelliest rides ever. I don't know who smelled worse – the camel or the guide. How I managed to wear that dress for days in Egypt and not end up smelling like a camel, I don't know.

I kept my hands on my hips most of the time to keep from perspiring under my arms. When I was in King Tut's Tomb, I smelled strong body odor and thought, "Oh no, it's happened!" But it was the man standing next to me. Somehow, I made it through with only one good dress and no body odor.

The Bedouin Nomadic Tribes in Egypt are so interesting. The values of our different cultures are so different. In America, we value possessions, but in the Bedouin culture, possessions are a

Riding "smelly" camel – wearing my purple dress

negative – they weigh you down. I have a fragile, primitive bracelet that I bought when I spent time with the Bedouin tribe. They pitch tents and travel by foot from place to place. They are all smelly and I understand why ... if you're in the desert and have a gallon of water, are you going to drink it or bathe in it?

In Cairo, I was crowded on the bus with people – the bus windows were knocked out. The people are volatile and emotional – no psychiatrists in that society. I finally asked my guide, "Have I seen everything?" He nodded. I thought to myself, "Good. Because I have no intention of ever coming back."

Africa

In Africa, I had the privilege of ballooning for the first time. It was like a religious experience – being in the small basket of a balloon as we floated over the migration of the Wildebeest, with 1000 of those animals running below in the Serengeti desert and the whoosh of the air in the balloon. I savored every moment of it. I was truly enchanted by ballooning and went several times later, taking Ivan with me. It was so thrilling to watch Ivan experiencing the balloon ride and all that came with it! I met a big balloon guy at NAS (Naval Air Station) Jacksonville, and we went up a few times. It's so awesome to be part of some 50 balloons all rising at once, which I did in Palm Springs. There was a Frenchman who was a big deal in La Chaîne, and considered himself so important that he always wore a three piece suit – not the best attire for a rough and tumble balloon ride! Balloon people are interesting and diverse. I remember once, in a small balloon – just the pilot and me – we lost altitude and landed in Ortega between two houses. Many wonderful balloon adventures come to mind as I remember back to those exciting days.

Russia

The CEO of Finn Air arranged a trip to Russia for our La Chaîne group in Philadelphia. The Russians were interested in starting a La Chaîne there and wanted to impress us – obviously. We were there for about ten days and every single meal – breakfast, lunch and dinner – was absolutely exquisitely prepared. I didn't realize we were under guard and being shepherded from one place to the other until I tried to get away from the bus for a nap...our guide went nuts. It was obvious she would be in trouble if she lost one of our entourage. There were only certain parts of Moscow and the rest of Russia that we were to see – and that was it. I took a nap on the bus.

Although our guide was concerned about getting herself into trouble, I learned later that she was not at all concerned about getting me into trouble. She had made arrangements with a doctor's wife in Jacksonville on an earlier trip to Russia that when the next person from Jacksonville visited, she'd slip an incredibly valuable Russian Icon in their luggage and send it to her. Just as I was getting on the plane, she told me she had put "a little something" in my luggage for her friend, this doctor's wife, and she gave me an envelope addressed to the lady in Jacksonville. I could have been arrested and thrown under the Russian Jail had anybody found out that I had in my luggage a valuable Icon that was never supposed to leave Russia. I've never been taken advantage of like that before. I was so unsuspecting that it never occurred to me that what I was carrying was contraband. I had just gone out of my way to be helpful. Duh. (It's a blonde thing!)

Finland

After leaving Russia, I stopped in Helsinki for a few days. I mainly wanted to see the whales off the coast and that was a quite a sight. The museums and the fabulous architecture were also something to see. Whenever I traveled, I tried to see as many of the sights as possible because I never knew for sure when or if I would return.

Paris to New York

I flew three hours from Paris to New York City on the Concord, and other than the flight attendant, movie star Shirley MacClaine and I were the only women on board. It was so expensive to fly on the Concord that only executive businessmen and celebrities could justify the airfare. That was one of the perks of being married to Milton … he could justify the airfare as a business expense and take me with him. I also traveled from London to Paris to Venice on the Orient Express and inadvertently got into the wrong room on the train. While I was taking a nap in the wrong room, everyone was going nuts searching for me, as they thought I'd been left in England when we crossed the channel.

As a model, I was privileged to travel the globe and be exposed to exotic and marvelous foods from many countries. Some of my favorite foods were discovered through La Chaîne, which also was the basis for many of my world travels.

Round Hill - Jamaica

Ivan and I spent a lot of time on the beach at Round Hill, which was a high-end resort for the very rich. Ivan was just three or four years old at the time, and as a long-time member of La Chaîne, I had exposed him to some really exotic food, including Uni, which is fresh sea urchin. The beach was full of sea urchins and the two of us sat on a towel in our bikinis and cracked open sea urchins and ate the still wiggling Uni with a spoon. People looked at us like we were crazy. Some people probably thought I was abusing the little boy, making him eat something disgusting like that. One American tourist came up and asked if he could try some Uni. He liked it and soon joined us. He ordered a good bottle of wine and we had a grand time – the three of us!

At Round Hill, we went to visit a Philadelphia couple at their beautiful home on the island. Their home had been featured in Architectural Digest – it was gorgeous and unique in every way – including guards with rifles on open walkways, due to the unrest that was happening at that time in Jamaica.

Alaskan Cruise

Ivan and I toured Alaska by ship, by ground and by helicopter. We landed on a glacier and went to Juneau and went whitewater rafting. What adventures we had together in Alaska and all over the world!

Navy Ship – Jacksonville to Baltimore & Back

I met the Navy Captain at Dwight's on Penman Road – we were both having Dwight's famous crab cake. We had a great conversation about the Captain's wife and four kids and our mutual friend, Admiral Delaney, whom I knew from the Hubbard House Board of Directors. At any rate, the Captain and I became friends and he called one day to invite me to take a cruise from Baltimore to Mayport Naval Station. It was after 9/11 and I had just returned from Las Vegas. I had an overnight bag packed, so I grabbed a cab and headed for the Jacksonville Airport. I had no idea what had been happening in the outside world.

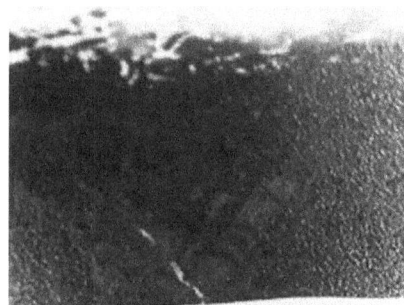

Ivan and me in Alaska!

111

When I got to Baltimore, the military policemen wouldn't let my cab through. I told them I was supposed to be on that ship – the U.S.S. Harry S. Truman – as a guest of the Captain. They verified that bit of information with the Captain and I was allowed on board. The cruise was from Friday to Monday and I shared a stateroom with two female officers. It was quite an experience. The Captain let me steer the ship and shoot the guns.

The Caribbean – La Samanna

Ivan and I were with Milton and family at La Samanna one Easter ($2,000 a night). We were at the pool and Ivan, about age 2, was playing with Robert

Haunts of the Very Rich

La Samanna, St. Martin

SIMPLE ELEGANCE AND SILKY SAND BEACHES FOR THOSE WHO LIKE IT HOT…AND PRIVATE

DeNiro's son in the water on Easter Sunday. Being a fairly new mother and not used to celebrating Easter with my predominantly Jewish family, I confessed that I had forgotten that the Easter Bunny was supposed to leave something for Ivan.

Later, DeNiro's son came to the pool with a big Easter basket for Ivan and said the Easter Bunny had left it at their room by mistake. That was such a nice gesture that I've never forgotten it.

Bike Trip to South Florida

Never one to turn down a challenge or the opportunity for adventure, I opted to accept the invitation to go on a bike trip to South Florida with a group of outdoorsy type people. I thought I was fit because I used to put Ivan in the basket and pedal around on the bike with Jason running alongside us. But this group was FIT!! The first day, I knew I was in trouble. An older woman was on the bike next to mine and she just casually mentioned that she'd just returned from a bike ride that took her from Portland, Oregon to somewhere in Virginia! Luckily, they took pity on me and although I was always last in line, they waited on me and someone would always come back and pedal with me. Somehow, I made the bike trip there and back … but never again!

Bus Trip to Georgia

Jacksonville historian Wayne Wood has organized some great trips on behalf of the Jacksonville Historical Society to places to observe architecture and historical relics. The last trip I took with Wayne and a group from the Historical Society was to the hometown of former president Jimmy Carter, Plains, Georgia. There, we were actually able to meet Jimmy Carter and his wife, Rosalyn at their church, and to hear Jimmy preach a sermon. It was a memorable and meaningful experience.

Bucket List Items …

I haven't ridden an elephant.

It is a delight to watch a busload of elderly Iowans run in the sand and surf at Amelia Island for the first time in their lives!
~ Iva Godiva Larson

11

ODD JOBS (AND I DO MEAN ODD)...

Over the course of my time back in Jacksonville, I have held many inventive occupations to make ends meet. Among them were hosting wine tastings, being a licensed mortgage broker, a travel consultant, a house-sitter, a Home Stay International coordinator, a limo driver, a landlord for a Bed & Breakfast ("Bed & Wine") apartment for Proton Beam patients, and a tour guide for St. Augustine, Jacksonville and Amelia Island.

I'm known by many friends as Iva "Godiva" Larson. I've spent a lifetime serving as an officer or board member on most of the organizations in Jacksonville, including the Jacksonville Symphony Guild, Arts & Advisory Board, Women's Food Alliance, Friends of Hubbard House, and more, and have been affiliated with Epping Forest Yacht Club, Ponte Vedra Inn & Club, The Florida Yacht Club and Timuquana Country Club and well as the Downtown Athletic Club in New York City. Having worked as an international model, travel consultant, mortgage broker, advertising executive, and restaurant owner, and retired from all of those pursuits, I started in early 2000 earning "fun money" as a tour guide of Jacksonville, Amelia Island and St. Augustine for Tour Time, Inc. I've learned that my hometown knowledge of Jacksonville and Northeast Florida, and the many amusing anecdotes I've heard along the way, are popular with tourists from far and wide.

In 2018, my sister Sue and I attended a fundraiser at the Cool Moose Café in Riverside for the Memorial Park Foundation and signed up for the silent auction and won the giclee (print) of that iconic photograph by Mark Krancer of the Statue at Memorial Park. It reminded us of those days long ago when we would go with our mother and have picnics at Memorial Park right in front of that same statue. What memories flooded back. There was actually a "Way We Were" column written about us in a local monthly, The Resident News. I tried to give my sister

IVA LARSON

IVA LARSON TOURS

Customized Private Tours

Jacksonville
Amelia Island
St. Augustine
North Florida
Coastal Georgia

Available as a "Step on Guide"
Using your group's automobile, van or bus
Or
Arrangements can be made for a full day or overnight luxury excursion
through my respected affiliate, Tour Time, Inc.

- You are invited to enjoy a versatile, authentic and often humorous glimpse of the areas' history, arts, industry and academia. As a Jacksonville native and life-long participant in North Florida's diverse cultural and commercial communities, I am uniquely equipped to share an insider's perspective with you.

- *Iva Larson Tours* offers a decade of experience informing and entertaining hundreds of visitors and newcomers to Downtown and Metro Jacksonville, Amelia Island, St. Augustine, and cities and attractions throughout Northern Florida and Southern Georgia.

- Tours are tailored to your particular interests, including but not limited to historical sites, local and international businesses, the areas' ecology, waterways and rivers, medical facilities, military installations, museums, schools, entertainment, shopping and fine dining.

- My business and cultural affiliations encompass Jacksonville Symphony (Guild President), Museum of Contemporary Art/MOCA (Board of Directors), Jacksonville Riverkeepers, Riverside Avondale Preservation, Proton Therapy Institute/University of Florida Shands Hospital (provider of patient lodging and guide services), International Gourmet Society, La Chaine (Jacksonville President), and Home Stays International (Area Director).

Sue the spotlight, since her life has not been as exciting as mine. I've always tried to be kind and considerate to Sue, but found out in recent years that she, like our mother, was jealous of the life I've lived and manifested that jealousy in disappointing ways. Unfortunately, since discovering some of the devious ways she has taken advantage of my generosity, I've had to distance myself from Sue and her family for my own protection. It makes me sad, but there's nothing to be done about it now, except remember the fun times – like being a tour guide!

Tour Time

For several years, I enjoyed working for Jim Uccio, who ran "Tourtime" bus tours. Jim used to always say that I made more than he did because people gave me such generous tips! I had a great time meeting people and entertaining them with historic and hilarious stories of all the places where I grew up. I realized, as being a tour guide came so naturally, that I've been a tour guide all my life. As a girl, I gave tours of the Children's Museum here in Jacksonville, and then when I worked for Prudential, I was chosen to show visitors around the building, and that trend continued when I was modeling in New York and I showed people around the UN. Meeting people and talking with them is enjoyable for me and has always come easily. I'm thankful for that.

Sadly, Jim Uccio passed away in May of 2021. He was a fine man with a great sense of humor and a passion for entertaining travelers to Florida. I miss him.

We used to go to NAS (Naval Air Station – Jacksonville) and tour the simulators and aircraft carriers. After 9/11, my tours of Mayport changed dramatically. All of a sudden, they brought dogs that sniffed the luggage on my bus. There was such a difference that it took a lot of the fun out of it. No more just waving us through the gate.

My car has been hit twice in the parking lot of Starbucks on Roosevelt by ladies backing up. Neither

Jim Uccio

of the times was it my fault. Last time it happened was on October 3, 2021, and as I was sitting in the Starbucks getting some coffee, I prayed it wasn't the same police officer who was at the scene when the young man in the truck hit me on Roosevelt and totaled my car! At the time of that accident, I wasn't injured miraculously, but my car certainly was. The young truck driver said, "I'll give you my insurance information," and I said, "We need a police report." Within a couple months of buying another car, a woman hit me in the Starbucks parking lot and I took her to lunch at Blue Fish and offered her a job. It wasn't a major collision, and I was looking for people to help me with tours at the time. We talked while we waited for the police to respond. She was a retired school teacher – seemed pleasant, but didn't think she could do the tour guide thing.

I loved giving those tours. I would have done it for free. Poor Jim, he passed away from cancer, but he loved doing what he did, too. If you love what you do you never work a day in your life. I love to make people laugh! On one tour, a man told me he'd brought a book along in case he got bored. He never opened the book. Giving tours is so gratifying. People hug you and tell you what a great time they had... and they give you a good tip!

Ritz Carlton – Concierge – 8th Floor

For a time, I worked at the Ritz Carlton, Amelia Island, on the 8th Floor – as a hostess for the rich and famous who came to the Ritz. They didn't know what to do with me, as I happened to know many of the people from Jacksonville who frequented the Ritz! My friend Gisela worked there and we had a ball together. I was the oldest person working there with the exception of the Cuban Janitor, but I looked good in the one-piece black uniform, so I got away with it.

At the time, I was into designing my own clothes. I had a friend in Avondale who had a dressmaking shop and I would bring her my designs to sew – the only stipulation being that I couldn't tell anyone I'd designed the dresses. I found some wonderful red material – satin with a subtle design – and created a strapless gown with a jacket.

I wore my red dress one evening when Flo Davis had organized a week at the Ritz Carlton for several movers and shakers in Jacksonville. Flo invited me up to her suite one night and I was wearing my red dress. As the concierge on the 8th

Red dress (with Ivan)

floor, I appropriated a bottle of champagne and headed for Flo's suite, but I got off on the wrong floor and knocked on the wrong door. There I was, standing at the door with a smile on my face, holding a bottle of champagne and wearing my knock-out red dress. A man answered and I knew instantly it was the wrong suite. He looked me up and down and said, seriously, "I'm SOOOO Sorry to tell you that you have the wrong room." It was obvious that he was REALLY sorry.

Employee training at the Ritz Carlton was like boot camp. Everything was done precisely, and it was not if, but when, there would be a fire. The first fire I experienced was from something hot being thrown in a trash can (probably a cigarette butt in an ashtray). I turned around and saw flames coming out of the trash can and I doused the fire with orange juice.

I probably worked at the Ritz Carlton for about nine months. At the time, I drove a Mercedes and I knew just about everyone in Jacksonville, so the guests were often friends of mine. I parked my Mercedes in the regular parking lot for quite a while until they discovered what I was doing and I had to start parking behind the Ritz in the employee parking lot.

Working at the Ritz Carlton was exciting, but I never really fit in. Sadly, the real Ritz Carlton is no more. It's been taken over by new ownership and they have junked it up to the point where it has lost its elegance. I took my friend, Keith Green, to the Ritz as a special treat for his birthday and I was so disappointed. There were game rooms and the place was so commercialized that I will not go there again.

At the Ritz Carlton
Craig Schoninger, me and Yvonne Corey

Voyager Club

At one point, I was employed by the Voyager Club, which was a boondoggle. A friend owned a travel agency, so I was hired to host cruises, which meant basically doing nothing and getting to cruise free – even being paid for it! How good is that?

MRI Job

Another job I had for a short time was as manager of physician relations for an MRI Firm. Again, I was the oldest person there, had no familiarity with computers or cell phones, and had never worked in a corporate environment. I visited the doctors (most of whom I knew) and turned in my expense report, which ended up being questioned by the manager in Jacksonville. He asked how I got such even numbers and I said I just rounded them off. The bean counter in California went nuts! I can hear them talking to one another, "Yeah, the blonde just rounded it off!"

Mortgage Broker/Realtor

Coplan put me in the mortgage business. I held mortgages on several properties on the East side of Jacksonville and when I went to collect the mortgage payments in these predominantly black neighborhoods like Soutelle Drive and Moncrief, the police at first thought I was looking to buy drugs. A white blonde in a Mercedes ...

what else could I be after in those neighborhoods? After a few months of coming on Sunday afternoons to collect the mortgage money, they got used to seeing me drive through the neighborhoods. It was a good business. I got my real estate license and still keep it current to this day. I was never afraid of going into those neighborhoods … I figured the bad people were too hung over to do anything and the good people had been to church on Sundays when I went to collect the mortgage payments. Most of them didn't have bank accounts, so they paid in cash.

Wine-Tasting

A neighbor in her early forties was doing wine tastings. She was immature, had poor judgment. She met this man who wanted to put her in a movie – she wanted me to drive down to the beach with her to meet him at the hotel. I asked her "Have you checked this man out?" She said he seemed fine. He wanted to put her in a movie. He wanted her to give him her driver's license. I told her to ask him to give her his driver's license. She did, and she never saw him again. Thank God she eventually moved back to Miami where her parents were. She needed supervision … and she wasn't even blonde!

One day she asked me if I could do a wine tasting, as she had two scheduled at the same time. I enjoyed doing it and have been doing it ever since. You can't make a living off of it. The pay is about $25 to $30 an hour for three hours. The people are in Tampa and they'll call and say they need me to go to Publix. I take throw-away glasses and a wine opener – they tell me which wines I'm going to be serving people. I read about the wines but it's really simple. You only have to know more about the wine than the people you're serving. The good thing is that I get to keep the wine I don't pour. Buddy Miller, who lived in the Cuckoo's nest (the apartment at Windsor Place) for years, used to love to help me empty my car after a wine-tasting – especially a Vodka tasting!

Limo-Driving

I was once hired by the Florida Times-Union to take a group of "Suit and Tie Guys" (important out of towners) on a tour of Jacksonville's "Good, Bad and Ugly." I took the guys to Biscotti's for lunch, and to several interesting historic sites. Finally, one of them said, "Iva, when do we get to the ugly?" So, I exited off of I-95 to the east side of Jacksonville on the back roads, and the first thing we saw was a dog-fight. Then, we drove a bit further and saw the ladies on the side of the road. I told the men that if the ladies had good teeth, they were probably undercover police – if they had bad teeth, they were working ladies. After a while, one of the men said, in a somewhat desperate tone, "Iva, could we go to the beach now?" I took them to Ponte Vedra Beach and then to Dwight's in Jacksonville Beach, where they enjoyed his famous crabcakes.

During the Super Bowl in 2005, I drove a stretch limo for Craig Smith, and had a great time. I always had baby aspirins and candy handy in my limo. Didn't want to have a diabetic that I couldn't take care of. I once took a course in CPR, but that didn't work out. I did things slowly (like we do in the South), and the medic pointed at my dummy and said, "Mrs. Larson, you've lost yours." I didn't lose any passengers during the Super Bowl!

I discovered that I could drive the limo just fine, and enjoyed it immensely … only one problem … I couldn't figure out how to back up that long automobile! One day I missed my turn to the Arena and made a U-turn which took up about six or eight lanes of traffic. I didn't want my passengers to miss the kickoff! A policeman was peering at me the whole time. I just smiled at him and waved and he let me do it. I thought he would swallow his whistle, but he didn't stop me. Blondes get away with so much!

Proton Beam – Bed & Breakfast (Bed & Wine)

I was at a luncheon one day and this man came over and asked if he could join me. He sat down and told me he had just finished proton treatment at the Proton Beam Institute. After learning that he was from out of town, I asked him where he stayed during his treatment. He said it was awful – a place in Springfield – but he had a dog and there was no place he could stay. I told him there was a party the next Saturday and invited him to come. I told him to bring his dog, which he had described as a Greyhound (I thought it was a miniature, but it turned out to be a regular sized Greyhound – Big!) When he walked in the door with his Greyhound, it was a bit of a shock, but the dog was very well behaved and quiet. He talked about being in Springfield where he was afraid to walk the dog and there were prostitutes on the street in the daytime – not just at night. He said he wished he had met me three months ago. He had finished the proton beam, but it made me think that I had this extra apartment – maybe I could rent it to proton beam patients. I was just eight miles away from proton and went over and took a tour – that's when I signed on to do the rentals for proton. They had a web-page and they did everything.

I used different names for my jobs, since I had so many going at one time. For Tour Time, I was Godiva. For Proton, I was Fran. For wine tasting, I was Iva. I still get calls for all three.

Proton beam people came from all over the world. There was a back up on occasion, when I'd have people in the Cuckoo's Nest and then I'd have to use the Windsor House, which had four bedrooms, for overflow. I had a lock and key on my bedroom door and an Angel on my shoulder. I know that the neighbors were convinced I was running a Geriatric Brothel, but it was all innocent and on the up and up.

I had proton beam guests at Windsor Place for 13 years and never had a problem with any of them. I charged $600 a month and they were there for three months. Their treatment was in the morning so they had no breakfast. They'd get home after lunch. I'd fire up the chimnea in the backyard and serve wine, cheese

123

and crackers. One guy loved to barbecue. He'd do the meat and I'd fix salad and dessert. It was like the Cuckoo's Nest, for sure, sometimes. A couple of guys fell in love with me, but I had my bedroom door locked upstairs. Once, I had a black couple staying there and the neighbors went ballistic. My tenants were all great. I had couples and singles and when the men were single, I'd take them to social events and try to keep them entertained while they were there. Some of them still keep in touch with me today. I remember there was one woman who drove up with her husband and when I came out to greet them, she took one look at me and yelled, "You're out of your F'N mind if you think you're going to stay here! Get your ass back in the car!" Obviously, they had some history.

And, speaking of having a history, Windsor Place has a history all of its own, and one of my proton beam patients, a man who was a police chief and a chaplain, painted this beautiful picture of the Windsor Place House and gave it to me as a gift.

When I was living at Windsor Place, I was always looking for gardeners. One day I saw a big grey-haired guy mowing the lawn next door. I went over and introduced myself and said, "I'm the neighbor next door. My name is Iva. What do you charge to mow a lawn?" He turned out to be an insurance executive who was mowing the lawn for his daughter, but he was interested in my offer. When he finished, he came over and I gave him a beer. His name was Dennis and I started paying him to mow my lawn. He didn't charge much. He pulled up in a Mercedes the first time to mow my lawn. Dennis told me one day that his daughter said all the neighbors thought we were an item, and I did go out with him, but it was not serious. He later bought a truck. Buddy, my good friend, was living in the apartment over the garage at the time and kept an eye n things. I had always tried to get my regular gardener to tear up the bamboo my neighbor had planted – it attracted snakes and rats and I was trying to get rid of it. Dennis had a machine and Buddy told him I'd been trying to get rid of the bamboo for years and he'd finally done it. Dennis was very protective. One day a couple of men stopped to talk to me. They were flirting and asking questions. Buddy was watching the whole thing and I didn't know that Dennis had walked up behind me. He had folded his arms in a menacing way and all of a sudden, these men backed off and drove away. Dennis was big and had the most beautiful blue eyes.

Buddy and Dennis and I went to a couple of parties. He looked great all dressed up, driving his Mercedes.

Miss Mumu (I called her) was a neighbor who watched constantly and called the police at every opportunity. One day, she called the police because Dennis's truck was parked illegally, in the wrong direction. The policeman came and pretended he was writing something and gave me a piece of paper. He said, "She is probably watching us and we have to respond to every call."

Once, though, I was redoing the garage and she tried to corner my housekeeper and find out what I was doing. I was paying the electricians and carpenters by the hour. I looked out and Miss Mumu was in the downstairs apartment asking questions. I'd warned them that my neighbors were nosy, but this was trespassing! I called the police and they rang Miss Mumu's bell. They said, "We've had a report you were trespassing on the Larson's property." She replied, "I didn't know she was home." Duh. Her husband was a Navy guy and Miss Mumu was pregnant all the time. He wanted to come over and play an album for me but I turned him down, rejected him. There were few bad neighbors at Windsor Place, though. Throughout my life, there were so many special neighbors. Pastor of Riverside Park Methodist, Dr. John Howard Hanger, lived across the street when I was in junior high. He wrote the following poem, titled Dogwood Days, about the street where we lived:

Now, Florida's a state to love … A land of sun and flowers.
In Jacksonville at springtime, Days slip by as fast as hours;
And there is no time nor season when they move at swifter pace,
Than when the Dogwood's blooming all along old Windsor Place.

Down the street and 'round the circle where Azaleas are galore,
There are moss-hung Oaks and Hickories shielding Redbuds by the score;
But when Redbud season's over, leaving not one pinkish trace,
Then the Dogwoods start their blooming all along old Windsor Place.

Here the spring is quickly over, and the street's not very long;
But where these two come together, it's as if they sing a song;

And the melody is lilting, and the words are full of grace
All about the Dogwoods blooming all along old Windsor Place.

We have never had a snowstorm, Snow and Florida won't mix;
For if it snowed, this city would be in an awful fix.
Yet each year we have a blizzard which all blemishes erase,
When the snow-white Dogwod's blooming, all along old Windsor Place.
If and when I get to Heaven (and I surely hope I will),

All that beauty will remind me of this street in Jacksonville;
For I sometimes think I'm looking Heaven squarely in the face
When all the Dogwoods fling their splendor all along old Windsor Place.

Man is forced to be alone by the very nature of society.
But if you meet a person who is not envious, who loves and believes in
<u>*other than himself, then*</u> *to this rare person offer a lifetime of friendship.*
~ Susan Polis Schutz

12

GOOD FRIENDS – THEN AND NOW

Maria Victoria Acosta-Rua

When I had cancer, Iva took me to chemo nearly every time. We would go by Whiteway and get my favorite sandwich and share it while I was having chemo. We laughed and talked and it went by very quickly. I felt sorry for so many others who were there alone with no one to be with them.

Gaston and I enjoyed being part of La Chaine and hosting dinners and going to them – it was fun to be in Iva's world of gourmet food. My sons, Fernando and Tony, loved the La Chaine events, too.

Once when Iva was married to Al Coplan, they went with Gaston and me to Europe. We flew from here to Paris, where my sister was having an art show and I remember we were walking in front of the Louvre and ran into Bob and Carol Shircliff and their grandchildren, and we all went to my sister's art show together. Guadalupe, my sister, is a talented artist and we all enjoyed the art show immensely. Ivan

**Maria Victoria and me
in Bordeaux, France**

127

stayed with Guadalupe and her teenagers and the rest of us went on to Bordeaux by train. We then got a car through Al Coplan, who told us to pretend we were press. We visited the Vin Expo in Bordeaux and tasted wonderful wines and we went to a vineyard there and had a beautiful visit as members of the press – we were treated to good Spanish ham and seafood – a gourmet meal with fine wines … just one of many trips we've made together!

"Iva and I have had many good times together – here and in Costa Rica and wherever we go. We are two extremely different personalities, but somehow we make it work. She is beautiful and kind and loves to make people laugh," said Maria Victoria, paying tribute to me - her dear friend of many years.

— Maria Acosta-Rua

Snow and Nam Nguyen – Lee Nails

Snow and Nam have been taking care of my personal appearance for many years – since shortly after I came back to Jacksonville in the early 1980's. They are a wonderful couple and I consider them dear friends. They are from Vietnam and say that they knew me before they could speak English. In fact, I used to make phone calls for them!

I called Lee Nails my Shangri La … where I could go and just relax in privacy. Their little daughter, Vy, used to do everything she could to disturb my peaceful privacy, thought. She couldn't keep her hands off of me. She loved my David Webb Bracelet. Vy got married a couple of years ago and I was invited to the wedding in Tampa. I didn't have a GPS in my car and got miserably lost. I think that's about when I decided to get an iphone with a GPS on it.

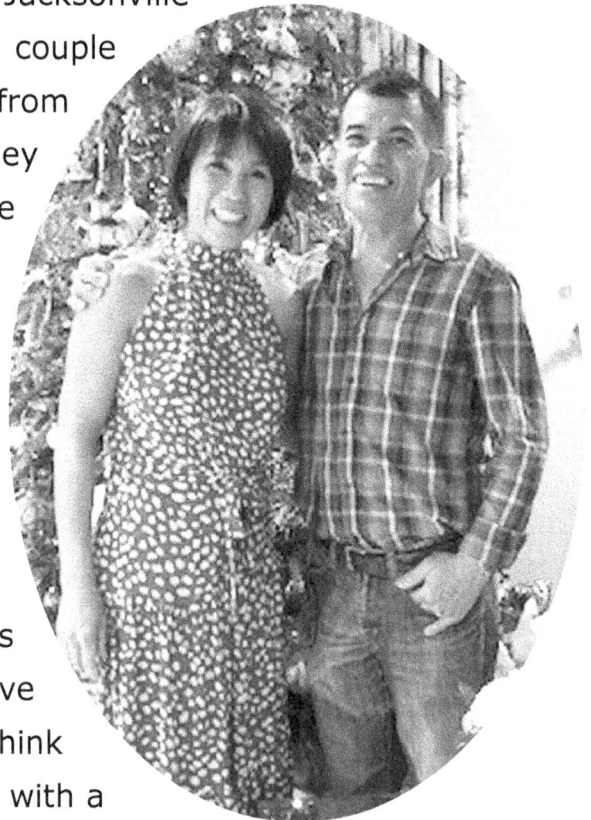

Snow and Nam

Reuben Keith Green

The two and a half years I had with Keith were some of the happiest years of my life. He is a unique and incredible man and I will treasure his friendship always.

I had seen Iva for years before I knew who she was, and I was fascinated by her. A few things we had in common: both of us were tall – both of us attracted attention – neither of us owned a bra. I had no idea she was an introvert like me. We met in the neighborhood, exchanged pleasantries a couple of times and she gave me her La Chaine card, but I didn't know her.

One day I was driving down Edgewood Avenue and saw her standing outside a furniture store. She looked distressed and it turned out she'd bought a bunch of furniture but didn't know how to get it back to her apartment. I threw it in the back of my truck and hauled it into her apartment. She invited me in for a beverage and we wound up talking for hours. That's when I learned that her first husband had been a Naval officer. We talked about her upbringing – my upbringing – my time in Jacksonville. We met again and it began to take a

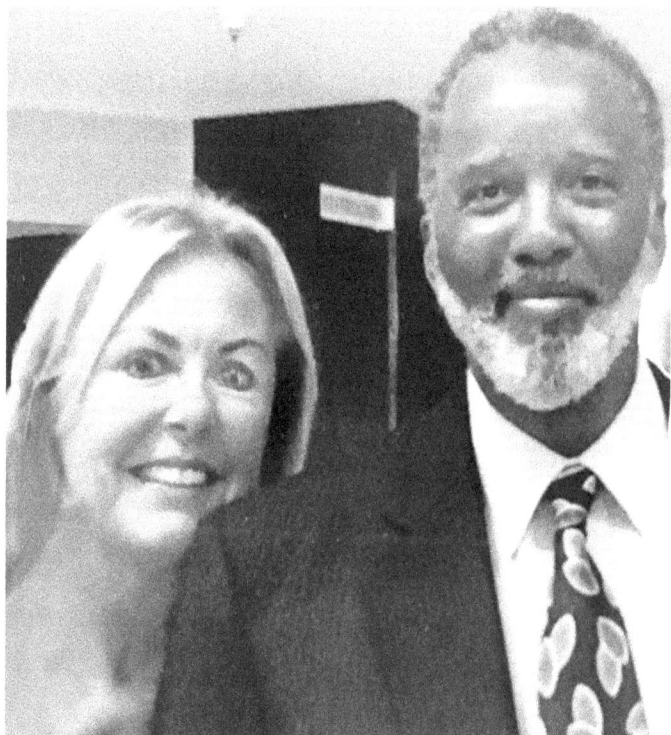

Keith and me

personal turn. I told her that I knew people would treat her differently if she was in my presence. I told her, "People will not view you the same if they see you're associated with me – everybody loves you and that may change if you're seen with me." She told me about her father having his house egged when they had African American guests and I thought to myself that it might have been bricks if they were dating one of the Larson daughters.

Iva hit the genetic lottery. She's tall, beautiful and smart – and she's *taken advantage of all that without being conceited. She is extremely self-confident, but not overbearing in any way. On the other hand, I was not a winner of the genetic lottery, but we both made bold choices with what we had. I left home at 17 with $20 and joined the Navy. I was an underdog with high ambitions and she was a beautiful young girl with high ambitions.*

Iva is probably one of the most empathetic persons I have ever met in my life – she treats everyone with kindness. She takes food and clothes to Memorial Park and hangs it on trees – it is a side of her that not many people know.

As far as our dating and going to parties, I watched people react differently to her when she was by herself or when she was standing with me. I remember a person who had been consistently nice to her until she was seen with me, and then he gave her a sarcastic snide response to something. I began to worry that my friendship would have a further negative impact on her – particularly as we got closer and closer. I always advised her on different approaches to things. I've traveled through life as a black man who looked over my shoulder and she's never had to do that.

Iva exposed me to lots of people I would not have met in this community – they see me in my coveralls and have no idea what my background is – what I did in my own life. There are not many black naval officers. The fact that I was an engineer in the Navy was something Iva found fascinating. The time I spent with Iva was wonderful. I was having issues after my writing my memoir – reliving experiences – and she was right there with me helping me through all of that.

She kept telling me that my story is unique and inspirational – and so is hers. What's important to share is not all the triumphs, but the adversities as well. Iva overcame a lot. She goes out of her way to hide her intelligence, but she's perceptive and intuitive. She does have a blind spot when it comes to people with bad motives or behavior, and she's very forgiving. On more than one occasion, I told her that sometimes you need to show people your fangs. There was a man she knew who had a reputation for being insensitive to black people –he was going on about his family and accomplishments and I commented to him that he was someone who was born on third base and thinks he hit a triple. He reared back and had nothing left to say.

One day, Iva called me very excited. "Keith, there's a submarine here at the Museum of Southern History that is a replica of the Hunley! I was telling them that my friend is a Naval Officer. Please come over and see this." They were buzzing around her, all excited while she waited for me. I showed up – they were in confederate uniforms and I could sense the hostility. I asked them what scale replica this was and they were curt. All of a sudden it became about race – it was interesting to see the drastic change in the dynamic and Iva was surprised. I was not. After all, I wrote my memoir on being a Black Officer in a White Navy – so their reaction did not surprise me at all.

Iva's son, Ivan, is fascinating to me. He reaches out periodically and thanks me for helping his mom. He's bought my book twice and obviously has read some of the stories. Ivan has had some real struggles. Unlike his mother's winning genetic lottery … Ivan has inherited some genetic misfires from Milton, in my opinion. Whatever is wrong with Ivan, I think he got it from his father, the sociopath.

Iva's landlord John joked with her when she moved in six years ago that he was going to have to have the street repaved if she kept sitting outside by the river. I enjoyed sitting there with her and watching the parade. We were told we were a striking couple … people actually stopped and told us that. Now that we are no longer dating, I continue to be her good friend and always will be. I never intend to abandon her. Sadly, I had to open her eyes about her family – it was painful for her to see what they were doing to her.

One of the best things about Iva was getting to meet her friends. I got a sense of validation from being invited to speak at the National League of American Pen

131

Wayne and Lana Wood with Keith Green

Women. The Navy has done its best to ignore what I've written about the history of African Americans in the Navy. More will be revealed.
— Keith Green

Paul Sifton

I met Iva through Maria's family – through Tony Acosta-Rua and his former wife. I met her in Jacksonville when Tony was on a trip. We are both members of MOCA and we kept running into each other at events and got to know one another. Then Tony was getting married in Costa Rica and we were both invited to the wedding. Iva asked if we could go together since I knew Costa Rica and the hotel and had connections. We had a wonderful trip together. At the wedding, I got to meet a lot of friends that I had never met before – on both sides.

One thing that Iva was doing was shuffling her feet and it would take her forever to walk any distance, so I got a wheelchair for her when we got off the airplane. I arranged for a wheelchair to pick her up in Costa Rica and she found out how lovely it is to travel and have someone push you around. She

had to be careful because she was in danger of falling – she learned that traveling perk and has used it ever since.

From what I know about her, she's had a flip phone for the longest time – didn't know how to do texts or emails and she got an upgraded phone and I showed her how to text and she became a texting fool – loading everybody with texted pictures and jokes because she had learned a new toy. Then she got on to email. I also got her set up on Delta so she would get points – so when she would go north to see her sons – she would ask me if I would book her flight for her – shortly after we got the Delta membership, I told her anything over $2 you put on your Delta American Express. She was so happy that when she wants to go to New York she can use her points and it won't cost her anything.

Paul Sifton

I knew Tony because I was living in Costa Rica and Tony was in the medical business in Costa Rica – we were both from Jacksonville – so people wanted to put us together. Tony and his wife were good friends – they lived in a condo that I had that was for rent – in the same complex where I was living – so we would get together frequently.

The Acosta-Ruas have a pig party once a year they do a big pig in Cuban style. I saw Iva there and she was surrounded by friends. She's got a tremendous lifestyle. While she's not very revealing, she certainly seems to have enjoyed some extravagant lifestyles with different husbands, different lifestyles. She's flamboyant and loves life. She seems to have managed her single life quite well. She enjoys the social life of going to art parties or to socialite type things and there was one event at MOCA that I was standing beside her and Keith Green was standing on the other side when all of a

sudden, she started to lose reality and her balance. I dropped my drink and tried to catch her – she went down on the ground and blacked out for a while and was taken away in an ambulance. I think that started her quest to find out what's wrong with her. She hit her head pretty hard on the ground – don't know what procedures she's had, but as you know, she's had an unknown ailment that is affecting her. They've finally ruled out Parkinson's – I don't know if they've pinned it down. She's an interesting woman.
— Paul Sifton

*Note: As I was being wheeled out of MOCA on a gurney that night that I fell so hard between Keith and Paul, I vaguely remember Wayne and Lana Wood coming in as I was "going out." They looked at me in shock and I felt like I had to say something, so I said, "Great Party!" Sometimes, my sense of humor under strange circumstances can come up with some zingers! This was one of them.

me with glasses

DK (Dinesh Krishnamurthy)

I usually go on my walk on her street and I saw her giving treats to the dogs – she's always at her window working on her book, watching the river. I've seen her many times and we began chatting. I run once a week all the way to Edgewood and back – she saw me when she went on her drive and stopped. She's extremely witty, humorous and jovial. She has fascinating stories to share from her life. Iva has known so many people. She talks about when her parents had a shop and she shares all the Jacksonville history with me. She is fascinating to me, sharing humorous incidents and adventurous travels. She makes it all very funny every time I talk to her. She always makes me laugh. For instance, some dude's car smashed into her and instead of worrying about it, she comes up with a witty remark

DK (Dinesh Krishnamurthy)

immediately. Once in a while, when I'm on my walk, she spots me and stops – sometimes she takes me on jolly-rides (she calls them joy rides) showing me where she used to live and things in Jacksonville. She's been a big help to me. I told her I hated to get my toenails done and she made me an appointment and took me to Snow at Lee Nails. There, I got my toenails done and it was fine. She also introduced me to Norma, who works for her and for John. Now, Norma works for me too, and she does a great job of cleaning. She also put me in touch with a good doctor for my checkup. Iva is a good friend to have. She's talking about writing her book – the history of her life – when she was in Africa and so many other places – I got interested and even designed a book cover. I can't wait to read her book!
— DK

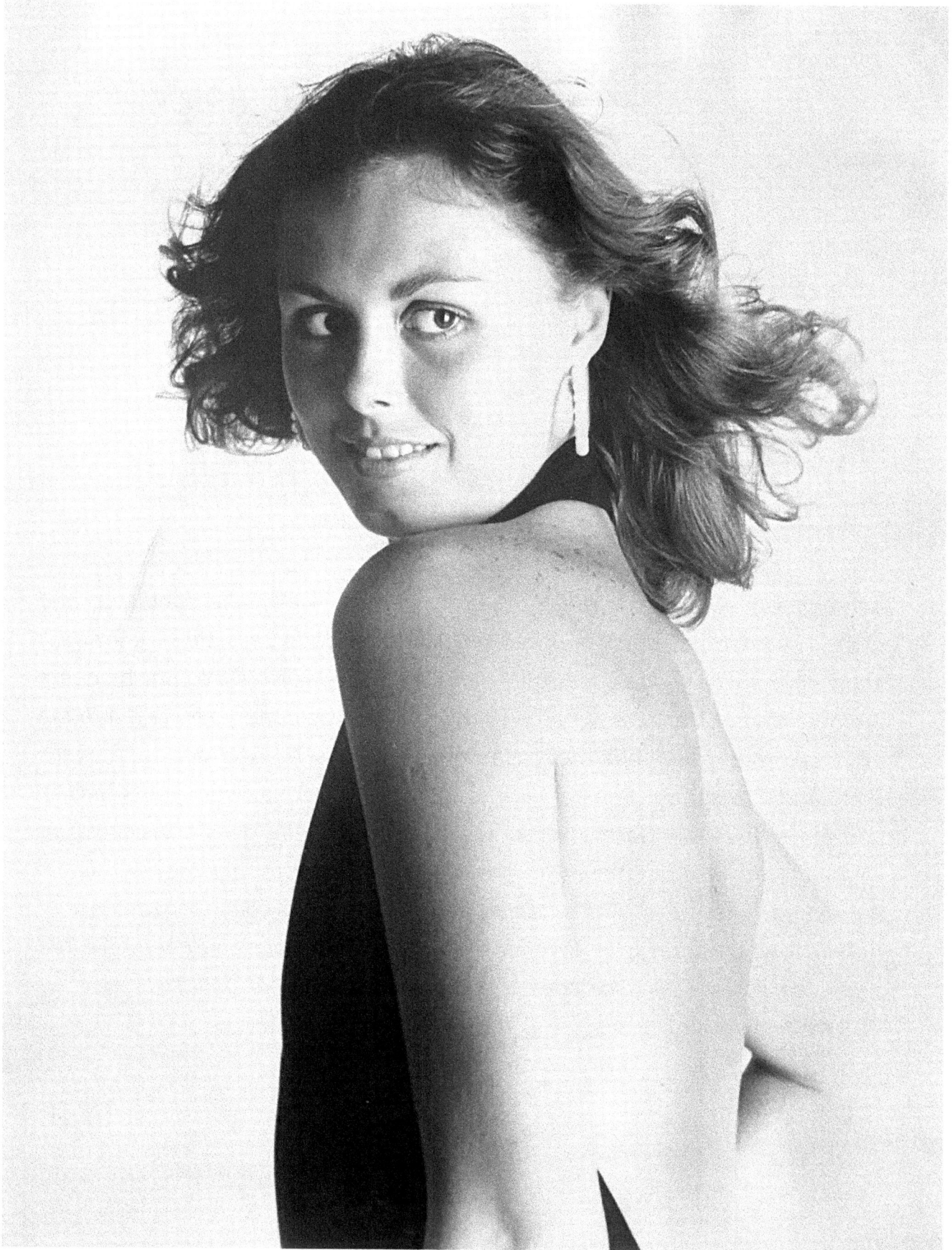

Betrayal is the only truth that sticks.
~Arthur Miller

13

ME TOO!

With the "Me Too" movement so prevalent in recent years, I made the decision to reveal some of the betrayals by males – past and present. It's amazing to me how many women have silently put up with abuse from men for years and are finally free to talk about it and call them out on it.

I was at the Blue Fish in Avondale in 2021, reminiscing with a couple of female friends about our days on the MOCA Board and the "Me Too" movement came up in conversation. Both of these friends – one prominent in the medical profession and the other a bank executive – revealed that they had been raped. That was one reason I decided to write about my "Me Too" experiences in this book. If people don't report it … it keeps going on.

There is a man here in Jacksonville who I've dubbed "The Christmas Creep." We've attended the same annual Christmas Party for years. It's a big party held at a beautiful home and the guests are like a who's who in this town. Every year, this dirty old man follows me from room to room until he can get me in a position where he can grab me from behind and put his hand on my crotch. No matter how I run from him, he always seems to be able to sneak up on me and do his deed, after which he chuckles gleefully and walks off – probably to accost other women the same way. Two years ago, I decided enough was enough and I reported him to the police. They assured me that what he was doing was sexual abuse. At the next party, I told him, "I've reported you to the police." He was indignant. "I only see you once a year!" he responded, not denying anything. Since then, he is glued to his wife's side at that party.

Years ago, when I was a single model in New York City, there was a really popular, good looking television news anchorman who asked me out for a drink in the afternoon. I'd been out with him a few times before, but that evening, I was unavailable. I had a dinner date with Michael McAllister, the youngest of the famous McAllister brothers who owned tugboats and had fabulous tugboat parties that were written up in the New York Times. So, I met the anchorman at a bar near my shoot and we had a drink just to pass the time before he had to go to work at the station and I had to meet my dinner date. I was still wearing the clothes from my shoot – a modest two-piece sleeveless, powder-blue suit, and I was walking with the anchorman when he pointed out his apartment building and suggested I come upstairs with him for a minute while he picked up his keys. By that time, I had some level of trust for him, so I said yes and accompanied him to his apartment. His doorman nodded as we walked into the building.

The minute we were in his apartment, he started kissing me and pushing me down on the floor. It was a violent attack. We were rolling around on the floor and I was fighting with all my strength. The fact that I was young and strong helped, but the thing that saved me was the model's girdle I was wearing under that plain cotton suit. These girdles were so tight, that we models joked that it could rearrange your ovaries! There was no way he could get past that girdle and as soon as he paused in his groping, I leapt up and ran out of his apartment. I was a shaky, wrinkled mess when I ran past the doorman and hailed a cab to take me to meet Michael McAllister. I was late and Michael was worried. I was never late. He saw me – trembling and wrinkled, visibly upset - and asked me what happened. When I told him, he was furious! He said, "I'm calling my two brothers and we're going to rearrange his face." I told him, "No Michael. There was no penetration and you and your brothers don't need that publicity. Let's just leave it alone." Reluctantly, he agreed.

That was back in the 1960's, you understand, and if a woman was attacked, people automatically thought it was her fault … that she probably lured him into it by wearing sexy clothes, etc. The doorman had seen me go in willingly and run out frantically – and the outfit I was wearing was certainly not alluring – so I might have had a chance of charging him with assault, but that was a different time and place, so I just left it alone. The kicker to this story is that the anchorman called me three days later and asked me out to dinner! "Are you out of your mind?!" I asked, as I hung up on him.

Models had quite a reputation for loose morals – drugs, alcohol and bad behavior. Lauren Hutton once asked me, "Would you fuck a snake for $1 million?" I was speechless. She got the $1 million contract with Revlon. Hmmm. That statement, in itself, shocked me. I was not the typical model ... in fact, I was then, and remained, a pretty naïve "Cowford girl."

Just do right. Right may not be expedient, it may not be profitable, but it will satisfy your soul. It brings you the kind of protection that bodyguards can't give you. So, try to live your life in a way that you will not regret years of useless virtue and inertia and timidity.
~ Maya Angelou

14

LIVES I'VE TOUCHED (MAYBE SAVED)

I knew Don Pearl through my late husband Edward Harry Duggan, Jr., an Admiralty Attorney. When he went out to see the ships, he'd get down in the bowels of the ships. He graduated from Annapolis, the Naval Academy and we met in Jacksonville.

Don Pearl was an Admiral's Aide in New York City in the Brooklyn Navy Yard and he and the admiral walked over the Brooklyn Bridge to go to the United Nations every day. At that time, to be homosexual in the Armed Forces, as Don was, and also to be that high up with the Admiral was completely unacceptable. The military police picked Don Pearl up and put him in a room with no legal counsel. They put him in a hospital out on Long Island. I didn't have money but somehow got in a cab and got out there and found that he'd been saving sleeping pills instead of taking them. Ed stayed in the reserves even after he did his four years. So he had a Navy truck and pulled up to the Navy Hospital where Don was and packed him up in the Navy truck and brought him to his parents' house in Brooklyn, New York – while I was talking to Don and Ed was finding us, he admitted he was going to commit suicide. I asked him for the pills. He said yes. We got him out of there that day. He stayed with Ed at his parents' house and I was living in the village. We found him an apartment just blocks away. He got a job with American Airlines and it was just perfect. He was in our wedding a few years later. Only one male alive who was in our wedding. His life ended up successfully. He came out and invited me to the gay parties. Men were dancing with men – Don was a fantastic dancer. He trusted me and let me see that part of his life.

At the Brick this year, a man came up to me and said, "Iva Larson. You saved my life. I'm alive because of you." He had too much to drink and was going to get in the car and drive back to the beach. I must have been living on Ortega Blvd., and I insisted that he sleep on my sofa. He did. He got up the next morning and drove back to the beach.

I was sitting out on the river on a pretty day in my bathing suit a couple of years ago. I've lived there for six years on River Boulevard and many people take walks along there every day. I thought I heard a man screaming and I got up and looked down the street and there were these two women walking and talking on their phones. The man said, "Help me! I'm drowning!" They didn't stop walking at all – they just kept talking on their phones. I got on my flip phone and called 911 and gave the location, telling them there was a man drowning. I knew I shouldn't go near him, as he might drag me down with him. I stood nearby and assured him that someone was coming and it was going to be okay. The policeman came and got down in the dirt and he was pulling this guy up. He pointed at me and said, "She was the only one who helped me." The policeman acted odd. He got the man up. I'm a hugger and kisser – he's telling the policeman … "She saved my life." I was going toward him to hug him. He said, "May I have the honor of shaking your hand."

The policeman knew he was one of the street people. What difference does it make? It's a human being. He had been on the bike, had put the bike down and gone over to look at the river and accidentally fallen in – didn't know how to swim.

True fame and fortune don't come from the outside.
They must be inside jobs starting with respect
and admiration closer to home.
~ Charles F. Glassman

15

FAMOUS PEOPLE I'VE MET

Christopher Reeves – I had a meaningful conversation with him. He was at a Jacksonville fundraiser that I was involved with. I am always early and there he was in his wheelchair. We had a lovely conversation. He told me how his relationship with his children was much more meaningful since he was paralyzed. Before, he played football and they were going and doing. Now they talked. How much closer and more meaningful his relationships had become! He was unassuming and down to earth. We talked for 30 minutes before things started. It was at the Times Union Building – across from the Omni.

No one ever said no to me about fundraising. People want to help. There was a man who had the Peter Pan Syndrome ... when you walk in City Hall, the first room on the right is named after him. I called him up because I was fearless. I have trouble asking for help for myself, but when it's a cause – Hubbard House, Humane society, Symphony, whatever, I'm aggressive. I called him and said, "Hi, it's Iva. I'd like to take you to lunch." He responded, "Iva, you don't have to take me to lunch. Just tell me what you want and I'll give it to you."

Gloria Estefan – I met her before she was famous. It was at a LaChaîne Pool Party in Miami. She was booked to entertain us. I've never been in awe of famous people, because they're just people. Never asked for an autograph. Manhattan is the size of Amelia Island and Manhattan probably has 4 million people – many of them famous - but we all put our pants on one leg at a time.

Having my hair cut next to Jacqueline Kennedy or Joan Rivers was a fairly regular occurrence. When you have your hair done at Kenneth's, he takes you back to your apartment. One day it dawned on me I was sitting in the back seat between Nancy Kissinger (taller than me – 5'10") and William Buckley's wife in a chauffeur driven limo – "carpooling" in pink mu mu's from Kenneth's. He gave the models a discount. He was smart. I'm sure the editor of Vogue went to him for free.

Grace Kelly and her son, the prince, came to a party when I lived in Haverford, Pennsylvania – she was on the mainline. When I married Milton, people would pay $150 apiece just to come see the house.

On the Philadelphia mainline, one of my neighbors was Leonard Tose who owned the Philadelphia Eagles and commuted in his private helicopter to and from work. That helicopter flew over our property – twenty acres. He gave me his private box for the KISS concert for Francesca, Jason and me. Jason still remembers the concert – all I remember is that it was very loud!

King Karl of Sweden – I had gone to Stockholm to visit my friend Johann Schard. I met him in New York where he was working at a law firm where my fiancé Ed worked. I took him under my wing in New York, so when I went to Stockholm, he picked me up at the airport. We had Aquavit (like Vodka) and Crayfish at a Festival and celebration and went right from the airport to the party – what a night that was! Johann and Prince Karl were both eligible bachelors in Stockholm. I went on a double date with Prince Karl and Johann. The women would have killed for Karl, who flirted with me and is now King Karl of Sweden.

Nat King Cole's Daughter, Natalie came to Florida Theater for another fundraiser. I picked her up and when I found out her mother lived in Marsh Landing, I called her mother and said, "I have a complimentary ticket and transportation for you to come and watch your daughter perform." Thank you, but no thanks!" she responded! Well, that didn't go well.

President Jimmy and Mrs. Rosalyn Carter. I sat next to Rosalyn Carter at church. After church, we went to their home. Rosalyn gave us a tour of the beautiful flowers and gardens on the grounds. She was quite gracious.

When I lived in the house on the Mainline, Conductor Zuben Mehta was our house guest.

Margo Fontaine and her husband in a wheelchair stayed with us. The reason he was in a wheelchair was that he had been caught with another man's wife, shot and paralyzed. I was cooking at that time and Margo told me she had to have a steak every meal because of her dancing … in order to keep her energy up.

I was probably 18 when I met Natalie Wood and Robert Wagner. They were on a train going to Miami and I was coming from New York. They were both very nice. I introduced myself and they were polite to me. I'd been on a trip organized by Prudential, after graduating a year early from Robert E. Lee High School. Prudential offered a trip to New York City. I stayed in the New Yorker Hotel and went to a Broadway Show. I slipped away and went to Powers Modeling agency on Park Avenue because I knew I wanted to be a model and that was part of the motivation to go to New York. They kicked me out because I had no photographs. Just a dumb kid from Cowford with stars in my eyes … no photos.

Live in the moment, enjoy the day,
make the most of what you have.
~ Michael J. Fox

16

BEFORE I FORGET COMPLETELY

I've developed some strong habits over the years as a model, a mother and a woman. For instance, I never posed for anything that I couldn't send home. I've had my own moral code – one that I was raised with – and I've done my best to live by it. Minding my own business is something I consider important ... "not my circus ... not my monkeys," you know? But that doesn't mean that I remain aloof when someone needs help. Having been taught from a young age to help others whenever I could, I still try to do that at every opportunity. I love helping people and I love people. Hate is not in my wheelhouse ... Hate destroys the vessel it's held in. I never harbor hate.

Giving back is nearly always more rewarding than expected. For instance, I once met a blind man when I was volunteering at the New York Library and I started reading to him. I took him home a couple of times and, as always, Ed welcomed him and even read to him occasionally. Ed always welcomed the "strays" I brought home. One day after we fed him and read to him, he asked to feel my face so he could see what I looked like. He touched my face and said, "I knew you were beautiful." What a lovely reward for doing good!

Eclectic Taste in Art – Favorite Artist Enrique Mora

He was a busboy in a beaches restaurant when we met. He'd put his art on the blackboard in the restaurant and I inquired about it and met him – liked him and his art! I bought my first painting that day in the parking lot and put it in the trunk of my car. Later, I had a cocktail party to introduce him around and his

reputation has grown to the point where I cannot afford his paintings!

I've never considered myself better than anyone else or anyone else better than me. I treated everyone with the same common courtesy and tried to instill that in the children. I've been happy that most of the friends who've been interviewed for this memoir have remembered that my parties were always filled with people who didn't look like me or like each other ... in other words, an eclectic mix of human beings just being themselves.

For all my life I've been blessed with good health and I'm gratified that I was in my 70's when diagnosed with what appeared to be Parkinson's disease but has turned out to be something that's probably worse. The doctors put a tube in my brain (called a shunt) to drain the fluid from my brain. I've always thought just being a blonde was a "brain

This photo of the International House in Philadelphia illustrates my philosophy of being simply one human among many.

drain" in itself, but this has now taken on a whole new meaning! The hospital experience at Baptist Hospital's Weaver Tower was unexpectedly pleasant. The staff treated me beautifully and I was in a private room on the 8th floor with a panoramic view of Jacksonville that included the river and the area where my apartment is located. I texted a couple of friends that my "sex-change" operation had gone well (Not really, just kidding ... but the surgery was a piece of cake and I'm hoping that this dizzy blonde will no longer be so dizzy now that the fluid is not clogging up my brain). So now, I am playing the cards I have been dealt to the best of my ability and adapting to my "new normal."

This book is part of my new normal ... sitting by my front window watching the world go by ... chronicling my life as a catharsis for myself. It is a mind exercise that continues to challenge me, and also presents an opportunity for those people who've always wondered about Iva Godiva! Now that I've gotten your attention, you know at least *some* of the rest of the story!

IVA-ISMS

While volunteering for Hubbard House in the mid-1980s, I was asked to appear as a speaker at a local corporation. When I saw that police were standing around, I asked why and that was when I was told that some audiences were not so appreciative of speakers on domestic violence - and that speakers had been attacked by men who felt they had been wrongly accused of being abusers.

Another time, Ivan's teacher reported that he was drawing everything in black crayon and she was concerned. I asked Ivan why he was doing that and he nonchalantly replied that the kids were seated alphabetically and with his last name Ross, black was the only color still available when it got to him.

Facetime phone call from Paul - I was taking a shower when the phone rang and I answered it, not knowing that Facetime was revealing more than my face! No more Facetime for me!

Ivan was often misunderstood because he came from such an unusual background. For instance, his school called to inquire about Ivan's "tall tales" of being with Mr. T. and Jackie Kennedy andRobert DeNiro's son ... all of which were true, as we had vacationed at a resort that was frequented by celebrities.

I've been known to attend the wrong Christmas party (wrong address) or - a classic - the wrong funeral. I was with Keith and we were going to my former housekeeper, Lena's funeral. We stopped at the first black church having a funeral - they didn't know what to do with me. For once, I knew how Keith felt in the middle of a white gathering. Finally, we discovered we were in the wrong funeral and went to a second black church nearby for Lena's funeral. Again, I was the only white person in the place. Finally, Kitty Crenshaw arrived. She knew Lena as well.

I was mistaken for actress Linda Evans at an airport in Canada. The woman was so insistent, chasing after me for an autograph, that I finally scribbled something and went on.

I was at a reception for Admiral Zumwalt and I thought he told me he had just gotten a sports car. I asked him what color it was. He looked shocked. He said it was gold. He had said, "Fourth Star."

A friend, upon hearing about some of my immediate family's misadventures, commented, "You were dropped off at the wrong house." Friends are the family I've chosen for myself.

The limousine business was tricky. Once I had to drive a limo up onto an Aircraft carrier. That was definitely not in the job description! And backing up was also a real challenge!

I once planted watermelon seeds in Daddy's rose garden.

M&R - Maintenance and Repair - are accomplished on me by my dear friends Snow and Nam at Lee Nails on a regular basis.

I dropped Jason off at Bolles and some boys saw me and asked him, "Who's that?" He answered, "That's my Mom! You're not going to hit on her, are you?"

Pheasant Hunt in France: What a hoot! I was in rare form and so were the pheasants!

Camp Blanding night maneuvers - I've seen them and they are scary.

Woman at Rockefeller Plaza asked me when I had a helmet covering my hair, "Are you a boy or a girl?" She said, "You be careful." I was speechless. Never been asked that question!

Cummer Couple commented on how well-behaved my children were. I told Jason what they had said, and he looked at me. "Do we have a choice?" he asked.

Make a Wish - terminally ill children got a limo drive - I had to keep my sunglasses on so they wouldn't see my tears.

Willis Paige - wanted to "Consummate our love." Give me a break!

Mrs. Peroni - poor English - we called her Mrs. Peperoni - we had just moved in and she knocked on the door and ran in and threw pennies all over for good luck. Every time I vacuumed, I would get pennies!

Chef Tell wanted me to pose for a photo with him - wearing just my apron! Not happening!

Bill Rice - had an MG Convertible with ironing board across the hood

Correct Street - Wrong House - Great Party! Happened often!

Where did I come from? Can you believe I came from Cowford?

When I first arrived in New York, the Jewish ladies wanted to know who did my nose.

They put Ivan in the hallway to eat his lunch - Sushi at St. Mark's

Miss Sedgefield was a time when women were not allowed to reach their full potential. I was booked for a limited time but without exception, I was booked for additional days.

Frank Sinatra's apartment - - Arnold Barsman bought the apartment but had to take all the furniture which he had no use for. Central Park West with a view of Park - 74th Street. I liked it!

Gold Club - Bank vs. Beauties - Limo - Cher and her sister, Dr. Phil, Ben Stiller - so many celebrities!

Daddy said, "I don't give a rat's ass what the neighbors think."

Dyslexia - not something I put on my resume.

The police car is a tomb, not a womb. I found that out dramatically while on a ride-around. I was the only one not wearing body armor!

I was a mortgage broker - from Moncreif to Ortega - you would be surprised at the people who are unable to qualify to borrow from the bank. I did no second mortgages - no commercial shopping centers, etc.

Ex-husband to be stalking me. I was sleeping in my car - it was a Mercedes, but it was still a car. During the day, I would attend board meetings with Haskell, Winston and Shircliff, and go to formal functions - then change in the lady's room and sleep in my car. No one knew - not Maria Victoria, my family or friends.

Chippendale - either furniture or dancers - depends on your perspective!

Returning to Jacksonville late at night years ago. I couldn't find a gas station and had to use the bathroom, so I pulled off the road not far from Camp Blanding and walked into the woods to do my business. Just then, a young man appeared from behind a tree. "Ma'am," he said, "I'm in a platoon doing night maneuvers. There's a soldier behind every tree." Needless to say, I ran back to my car and drove home as quickly as possible!

I was locked out on the balcony of the Ritz Carlton on the 8th Floor where I was working as a concierge. I knocked and waved, trying to get people's attention, and I did ... they just smiled and waved back!

I was locked in while at the Ritz Carlton, too. I had the 7 a.m. shift and went down to the basement freezer. We had four food presentations and I needed to pick up some food for our first shift. The freezer door closed behind me. I nearly froze to death before someone heard me pounding.

I was on a plane just about to land when the pilot announced there was a problem with the landing gear. He was circling the airport trying to get rid of gas in case we had a crash landing. Somehow we landed safely, but you know it's not a good day to be in an airplane when you look out the window and see emergency vehicles and foam on the runway.

Lucy Ricardo has nothing on me! I love to make people laugh.

I wanted to go into the Peace Corps - I chose modeling instead. I think I made the right decision!

Letitia Baldridge asking me for advice? Crazy and flattering.

Children came to visit. Francesca asked, "Where's the rest of the house?"

Ivan, age 3, asked a priest with a robe - "Do you have a vagina?"

Woman hit my car - we talked while waiting for the police - Later I took her to Blue Fish for lunch and offered her a position as a history tour guide. She was a retired teacher.

A child once inquired, "Is a giraffe as tall as Iva?"

May Day - May Day! Anchor slipped at Bitter End in the Islands.

Girl Scout - always be prepared. Baby Aspirin and candy in my purse.

Well, I did it again. I've been watching my next-door neighbor and he put down sod and maintains it beautifully. He maintains his car and takes care of another car, so I approached him about detailing mine. He said he would be happy to do that. I thought he had a detailing business but the car was his daughter's and he owns a corporation! Another Dennis story - cutting my grass!

A man who always saw me in the window saw me in Publix one day and said, "Oh, you have legs!"

Daddy always came home for dinner with our family and then returned to work.

The lady at therapy said, "I want to sit right here and read your book!" She had to double up on her next client because my book took up most of my therapy time.

s In Auto Insurance

are made grudgingly, half a loaf at a time. That's history.

The average buyer of auto insurance yearns for several common sense improvements. One is a uniform, utterly simple system of rates for auto owner-drivers enabling them

to shop with ease as the philosophy behind the California Plan contemplated. Another is compulsory insurance for all drivers, bar none — no cancellations, but sky-high rates for bad drivers — with every tub resting on its own bottom.

Then there is the idea of a rebate at year's end to reward the driver who's done a good job. And, of course, the immediate-pay plan as a means of cutting back on law suits and eliminating a pet gripe of policyholders.

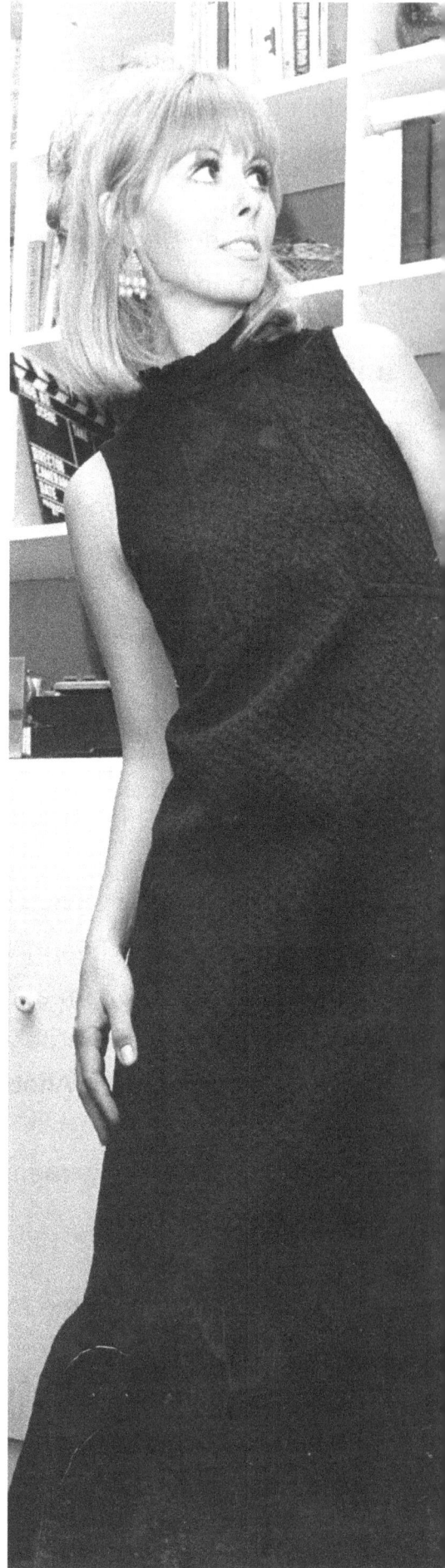

Ivan and Jason with their dad, Milton

II

LETTER FROM IVAN

Mom,

The past few days have been a lot of fun. Also, I wanted to thank you for your unconditional caring and support over the years. Your own will and determination always accompanied by a smile and optimistic take on life has been a wonderful influence.

Happy Mother's Day,

Ivan

III

ACKNOWLEDGEMENTS

In 2021, the stars aligned, and I was finally able to write the story of my life - a project which had been suggested to me by many over the years. I am grateful to several good friends - one in particular who bought me several books and a tape recorder for my biography. Others, who know who they are - too many to name - encouraged me to do this book. And to my friend, Biographer Susan D. Brandenburg who agreed to meet on Sundays and make it happen - this book could not have been done without you.

With hugs and love,

Iva Godiva

March 2023